# TABLE FOR TWO

### THE ALL-IN-ONE HEALTHY PREGNANCY & FOOD GUIDE FOR EXPECTING MOM & BABY

## ELIZABETH NEWBORNE

# CONTENTS

## 14 Baby Essentials Every Mom Must Have...

*This checklist includes:*

- 14 ESSENTIALS THAT YOU DIDN'T KNOW YOU NEEDED FOR YOUR LITTLE ONE AND YOURSELF
- ITEMS WHICH WILL MAKE BEING A MAMA BEAR EASIER
- WHERE YOU CAN PURCHASE THESE ITEMS AT THE LOWEST PRICE

The last thing you want to do is be unprepared and unequipped to give your little one an enjoyable and secure environment to grow up in. It is never too late to prepare for this!

*To receive your free Mommy Checklist, visit the link or scan the QR code below:*

https://purelypublishing.activehosted.com/f/1

## INTRODUCTION

You just found out you're pregnant, and now you're completely overwhelmed by a mix of excitement and anxiety—especially if you're a new mom. Growing a life in you is a remarkable experience, but it comes with a lot of uncertainty and worry. I know, I've been there, and I spent countless hours reading pregnancy books and scouring the Internet for answers to all the questions whirling around in my head.

I'm sure you started doing research as soon as you got a positive pregnancy result, and you've come face to face the mountains of information—a lot of the time with conflicting advice—all around you. It's hard to know what the best approach to pregnancy is when it seems as if no one can agree on one!

This book is based on the most up-to-date scientific research regarding prenatal, perinatal, and post-partum care that will lead to a healthy baby with a happy mom. But I will also share with you the knowledge I gained through my three pregnancies. And believe me, I learned something new each time. I want to take the guesswork out of caring for yourself and the little one growing in you by combining the most beneficial information in one place. It doesn't matter if you're a first-time mom or if you have your second or third baby on the way; this book brings together everything you need to know to have a healthy and happy pregnancy.

It's going to be a journey, and I will walk it with you. We'll start by making sure you have a positive mindset, free of any fear and unnecessary worry. Well, as much as possible—moms always worry. It starts as soon as you learn you're growing a tiny life, and I don't think it ever ends.

I'll also share with you how to eat healthily throughout all trimesters to help your baby grow strong. The fact that I am a nutritionist made it easy for me to know what foods to eat and those to avoid, but that's not a luxury most women have. New moms also don't always have the funds to visit a nutritionist to help them understand what is right for them and their babies. I am here to help, and I am glad that I'm able to share my knowledge with you.

Most of the advice you'll find online is well-meaning, but regrettably, is often outdated or not based on the most recent scientific findings. In *Table for Two*, all the recommendations I make are backed up by research, so you can be a hundred percent confident that the food and lifestyle options in this book will support a healthy pregnancy.

All-in-all, I want you to walk away feeling confident enough to carry through your pregnancy effortlessly and with a sense of calm. I honestly wish I knew everything written in this book when I was pregnant the first—even the second— time.

Some common subjects I'll address, and questions you'll have answered in *Table for Two* include:

1. It is my first pregnancy, and I am unprepared. I am scared.
2. What should I eat to make sure my baby is healthy?
3. There's so much information out there, who should I trust?
4. I'm terrified of losing my body in the process, and what about my mental health?
5. What if I get depressed after giving birth?

These are only some of the pressing issues I will be covering in this book—a new baby means a lot of changes are about to happen, but we'll go through it together. I know there's another matter you're not sure about as well: when to tell others.

Although that is entirely up to you, a lot of women wait for the first trimester to pass before they share the news with their family and friends. The reason why they do this is somewhat morbid; they keep their pregnancy quiet in case of a miscarriage. On the one hand, I can understand why some may feel this is the best way to do it—it will lessen the trauma of having to inform a lot of people if your pregnancy takes an unfortunate turn. But then again, I would think the support of friends and family will be invaluable during such a time. As I said, it is your and your partner's choice, and you don't have to do it one way or the other because someone said so.

Starting now, I want you to take care of yourself. Your own health and what you put in your body affect the tiny one in your tummy. Always think of it this way: What is good for you, will be good for the baby. So, eating the right foods, exercising, and leading a stress-free life is paramount to the health of both mom and baby.

A lot of people are involved in helping you have a healthy pregnancy—doctors, nurses, midwives, and other support staff. They will be there for you every step of the way, and so will I.

Before we move on to Chapter 1, I think we should get a little scientific.

## A Boy or a Girl?

I've always been fascinated by genes and their ability to determine a baby's sex, hair and eye color, height and build, as well as blood type! I remember when I first got pregnant, I did some research because I wanted to know precisely how the body makes a boy or a girl. In case you're also wondering, here's how it works.

An average human cell is made up of 46 chromosomes, but male sperm and female eggs only contain 23 chromosomes each. As fertilization takes place, the 23 chromosomes each of the mother and father pair and make 46 in total. These thread-like structures carry around 2,000 genes, which we know define a person's inherited physical characteristics.

When it comes to the sex chromosomes, a fertilized egg will have one from each parent. The one from the mother's egg is known as the X chromosome. The sex chromosome from the father's side can, however, be either an X or Y chromosome. So, if the chromosome from the dad is X, the baby will be a girl (XX), and on the other hand, if the sperm contains a Y chromosome, you're expecting a boy (XY). Interesting, isn't it?

**What About Twins?**

Multiple pregnancies can either lead to fraternal twins, triplets, or more, or identical twins, triplets, or more. The main difference lies in if one egg is fertilized and then split (identical), or if multiple eggs are released and fertilized (fraternal). Fraternal babies are much more common than identical twins. In fact, two-thirds of multiple pregnancies are non-identical, while a third is identical.

You have a one in 10,000 chance of having triplets naturally, and the chances of having quadruplets are even rarer. However, if you go for artificial insemination, your chances of having multiple babies increase significantly.

These signs may point to you carrying more than one baby:

- You get morning sickness very early in the pregnancy.
- Your belly is bigger than it should be in relation to how far along you are.
- There are twins in your family.
- You've had fertility treatment.

You will know for sure when you have an ultrasound scan between eight and 14 weeks. The doctor will also be able to tell you if the babies are identical or not—if they have separate placentas, they can be either identical or fraternal, but when they share a placenta, they're always identical.

Now that I've shared some noteworthy information with you, I think it's time to jump into Chapter 1 and discover how the right attitude can help you get through your pregnancy with your sanity intact.

## CHAPTER 1: A HAPPY MINDSET
## LEADS TO A HAPPY BABY

*a*s a soon-to-be momma bear, you have to make sure your mind is in the right place. If you approach your pregnancy with a mindset that is positive and based on self-care, you'll be more present during this extraordinary time of your life. Fear of the unknown can suck all the joy out of you, and that is the last thing you want when you're growing a human inside you—there is already enough physical discomfort to deal with.

I know you may be worried about the health of your baby, the process (or rather, the pain) of giving birth, and everything that comes afterward. Mindfulness can help you cope with these fears. But what exactly does it mean to be mindful? Well, it's the ability to be aware of your emotions in the present moment without letting them drown you. It is when we shift our focus away from the present but to the future that we start to dream up worst-case scenarios and make ourselves sick with worry. By practicing mind-fulness, you'll be able to manage your anxiety, and it may even help alleviate any aches and pains (Duncan et al., 2017).

If I think back to when I was carrying my first child, I had this constant knot in the pit of my stomach caused by worrying about everything that could go wrong during labor. Of course, the stories of how painful childbirth is didn't help. It was only after I joined a birthing class and met a woman on her second pregnancy that I was able to calm my nerves.

She taught me how to stay anchored in the here and now. This was essential during my pregnancy, and as I was giving birth. For one, studies show that women who are afraid of childbirth will have to endure labor for longer—anywhere up to 50 minutes longer (Adams, 2012). Considering that it took my first child 16 hours and 34 minutes to come into this world, I will pass on adding close to another hour to that, thank you. I'm sure you would, too.

For your emotional well-being, during and after pregnancy, I can't recommend mindfulness enough, especially if you're fearful of giving birth. It teaches you that labor isn't only painful contractions, but that there are moments of reprieve that you can fill with calmness. It also helps you discover that you're stronger than you realize; you just have to manage stressful situations moment by moment.

Furthermore, mindfulness will help you adjust to your new role as a mother, which will help you manage any hopelessness and despair that may arise.

The fact of the matter is, you won't be a glowing ray of sunshine the entire 40 weeks of your pregnancy.

You'll have to deal with negative thoughts, doubts, depression, and anxiety—not to mention the physical aspects. Finding something to ease some of these symptoms is necessary for you to stay sane, and mindfulness may be just what you need. Also, if we take into account that stress and a negative mindset may get in the way of the mother and child bond, as well as interfere with your baby's development, destressing is just as important as going for regular check-ups and drinking your prenatal vitamins (Vieten & Astin, 2008).

If you're still not convinced, here is a breakdown of four significant effects of mindfulness on mom and baby.

## MINDFULNESS REDUCES STRESS

Mary, a friend of mine, recently had her first child. Unfortunately, there were some complications, and she was put on bed rest for two months before she was due. As you can imagine, this caused a lot of extra stress, and to make matters worse, she couldn't do mild exercise to combat her anxiety. I told her about the mindfulness techniques I used when I was pregnant. She ended up taking it a step further and started to include breathing meditation, as well as body scan meditation in her daily mindfulness routine. She couldn't stop talking about how much more at ease she felt.

Studies corroborate Mary's positive experience. In 2008, two researchers set out to prove the advantages of mindfulness practices during pregnancy. They found that women who practiced only two hours of mindfulness a week reported a reduction in stress levels, as well as negative feelings such as distress and hostility (Vieten & Astin, 2008). Another study focusing on 19 pregnant women found precisely the same thing—mindfulness reduces stress and depression (Dunn et al., 2012).

It's all about being able to stop, take a breath, and calm down.

The constant worry and nervous tension tend to be worse in your first and second trimester. The feelings that you experience during this time—or at any time during your pregnancy, actually—are called "pregnancy anxiety." Pregnancy anxiety describes a loop of worries that get triggered by the most random events. You may have an ache in your right upper leg, and your brain will immediately think, "Something feels wrong, the baby is in danger," and you'll end up in the emergency room. This overreaction to the tiniest of things isn't healthy for you or the baby. Mindfulness gives you the tools to handle these complex emotions.

## MINDFULNESS MAKES YOU MORE POSITIVE

When you think mindfulness, you probably think meditation. But that's not all there is to it. It's also the ability to be mindful of your moods and what physical sensations you experience during the day. The reason why paying attention to daily experiences is important is it makes it possible for you to recognize not only the negative aspects of pregnancy, but the joyful moments too. A lot of the time, pregnant women get so caught up in the swollen feet, nausea, and all the other unpleasant parts of growing a baby, that they forget the little delights of preparing the nursery, seeing the baby on the sonar for the first time, or feeling that tiny flutter of a kick.

In 2016, a group of pregnant women were trained to pay attention to the small things. They were then asked to write in their diary twice a day and explain how they felt both physically and mentally. This small task made it possible for them to see how much their moods and physical health changed throughout the day (Zilcha-Mano & Langer, 2016).

These women noticed an increase in feelings of contentment, enthusiasm, and determination, as well as an improvement in their general well-being. There was a marked difference between this group of women and the ones who only read about other women's experiences instead of being mindful of their own.

Furthermore, the women who practiced these mindfulness techniques were in better spirits after birth, which is a good thing seeing as you need all the help you can get during this time.

MINDFULNESS MAY PREVENT PREEMIES

Preterm birth is possibly one of the biggest worries you'll have when you're pregnant. Babies born before 37 weeks—called preemies—are at risk of various health conditions, including breathing problems, impaired vision, and overall developmental delays (Centers for Disease Control and Prevention, n.d.). The mothers of preemies have to deal with a lot of extra anxiety and stress, which most of the time leads to depression (Segre et al., 2013). What makes matters worse is that the baby's needs overshadow the emotional distress of these mothers.

Mindfulness may reduce the risk of preterm birth, according to a 2005 study, where half of 335 pregnant women were asked to meditate and practice yoga for an hour a day, while the other half only went for a walk (Narendran et al., 2005). The group who practiced mindfulness had fewer preemies, and their babies were born at a healthy weight.

Then there is the Apgar score (appearance, pulse, grimace, activity, and respiration), which is measured minutes after birth. There is a definite link between mindfulness and this score if we look back at the 2016 study done by Zilcha-Mano & Langer, mentioned earlier.

Your pregnancy care team may very well recommend mindfulness practice, especially if you're at high risk of giving birth to preemies.

## MINDFULNESS MAY HELP THE DEVELOPMENT OF YOUR BABY

The studies on the impact of mindfulness on early development are very promising. In 2015, researchers discovered that mothers who practiced mindfulness from the second trimester gave birth to babies with fewer developmental problems. The mothers who participated in the study were asked to report daily on their child's adaptability and overall behavior.

They found that these babies settled down and adjusted to new environments with ease, and they had the ability to control their attention and actions (Van den Heuvel et al., 2015). For example, these babies would calm down faster after a bout of crying and would be more likely to avoid touching things they were told not to. The stress-beating effects of mindfulness had a notable impact on boys, with self-regulation being the leading outcome.

Moving on to other developments, babies of mindful mommas could distinguish between repetitive and unusual sounds (Van den Heuvel et al., 2015). This indicates that these babies are capable of dividing their attention to sounds at a young age, which means learning language will come more naturally to them.

## 4 TIPS ON HOW TO BE MORE MINDFUL

Now that you know some of the benefits linked to mindfulness during pregnancy, here are four tips to help you get started.

But, before you do, remember that mindfulness needs to be practiced—day after day. It's actually like parenting to a certain extent; you continue to work on it even if some days are horrible, and you feel like you're not doing anything right. It can be tedious at times, but keep your ultimate goal in mind: a happy and relaxed mommy leads to an easy-going pregnancy, of which the end result is a healthy baby.

## SLOW DOWN

Take your time—you will never have as good an excuse to slow down as you do when you're pregnant. Don't over-schedule activities and always make some time for yourself. You will appreciate the fact that you didn't rush anywhere while you were pregnant when you have strollers, carriers, car seats, and untimely diapers to deal with. Take time to breathe; your body will thank you. It's also good to remember that your baby—whether they're in or outside—will know when you're feeling anxious. Your worry will rub off on them, and that is not fair to your little one.

## IT IS WHAT IT IS

There's nothing wrong with researching how you want to give birth—it's always advisable to make an informed and conscious decision. But make peace with the fact that things don't always go according to plan. Childbirth doesn't run on a schedule or according to a set program.

You may decide on a home birth, only to be forced to change your plans at the last minute for the safety of you and your baby. When this happens, take time to acknowledge the change and deal with it mentally and emotionally—even if you only have a split second to spare. If you cover up the disappointment you might be feeling, it will make it difficult for you to bond with your newborn. Take a breath, tell yourself that everything will be okay as long as you give birth to a healthy baby, and then let your dissatisfaction go.

## SLEEP ENOUGH

I cannot emphasize this enough—a good night's sleep will make a huge difference. But, have you ever heard of a pregnant woman who could get eight hours of uninterrupted sleep? No? Neither have I.

I remember I had to take naps during the day to make up for sleepless nights. After giving birth, the struggle continued with regular feedings, nappy changes, and overall restlessness due to regularly checking in on the little one.

I started doing a body scan when I wanted to fall asleep, and it worked so well, I was upset that I didn't know about this technique while I was still pregnant. To make sure you get as much shut-eye as possible, here are the instructions for doing a relaxing body scan.

1. Start by becoming aware of the weight of your head and pay attention to the various muscles in your face.
2. Move down the length of your neck, your shoulders, and down your arms. Feel the weight of each body part. Stop at the palms of your hands and feel the sensation of heat radiating from your palms and fingertips.
3. Focus on your breath as it fills your chest. Feel your ribcage expand and contract as you breathe in and out. Imagine the air

flowing around your baby—nourishing
them with each breath you take. Keep your
attention here for a moment, then start to
move down your body.

4. Feel the weight of your hips, then legs.
   Continue scanning all the way down to
   your toes until you can feel all parts of your
   body as a whole. With each breath, let your
   body sink more deeply into the bed,
   relaxing all your muscles.

After doing this exercise, you'll hopefully fall asleep without any trouble, and if you don't, you'll still benefit from taking the time to relax.

## DON'T TAKE A RIGID APPROACH

Once your baby is born, you will have to change your mindfulness practice. The keyword there is "change," not stop. If you try to keep to the mindfulness schedule you had before giving birth, you'll end up feeling like you failed because you couldn't stick to it.

You won't have time to do two hours of yoga a day anymore, but that doesn't mean you can't fit in 10 minutes of stretching when your baby is taking a nap, and another 10 minutes when they're peacefully playing. You have to be flexible with your time when you're a mom. However you do it, just keep practicing mindfulness. It will keep your energy levels up and encourage a positive postpartum outlook.

## YOUR MENTAL HEALTH IS KEY

A sunny outlook on life is the best way to live, but even more so when you're expecting. We already covered some of the worries most pregnant women face—ranging from finances, to being a good mom, to fretting over the health of the life growing inside them. These are normal reactions to such a life-changing event, but the best thing you can do is to give more weight to the positive.

It's no secret that anxiety and a negative mindset take an emotional, mental, and physical toll on you. However, if you can cultivate a "glass half full" attitude, you'll lessen these adverse effects on your well-being. I'm not saying you should bury your head (and feelings) in the sand, but to stop focusing on the negative aspects of being pregnant—even if just a little. It's not about ignoring the changes you're going through, but instead learning how to handle the stress. A positive attitude, getting enough sleep, exercising, and eating a healthy balanced diet are ways you can manage negative feelings. Meditation, prayer, and talking to someone will also help lift your spirits.

I find positive self-talk makes a big difference. When you change "I can't do this" to "I can do it," you become mentally stronger and more resilient.

Here is some negative internal dialogue you should stop in order to have a healthy and happy pregnancy.

 *"It's too late to change unhealthy habits, I'm at the end of my first trimester already."*

It's never too late to give your baby the healthiest start possible. If you stop smoking, drinking, and using drugs, your pregnancy will have the same outcome as mothers who didn't have any of these bad habits (Hedderson et al., 2016). Of course, the earlier you quit, the healthier you and your baby will be.

 *"I have no one to support me."*

Having a "tribe" to carry you through your pregnancy will make the process much more bearable. This doesn't mean you should fall into a negative mindset when you don't have family and friends to support you. You can start to create your own circle of support as soon as you find out you're expecting. Prenatal yoga classes, childbirth education groups, and even churches are great places to meet other moms who may themselves also need extra support. Reach out to them and start building your own tribe.

> *"My parents were horrible. I just know I'm going to be a bad mom too."*

That is a very negative mindset that will consume you. The fact of the matter is, you will be the mom you want to be. I know it is unnerving to know that you will be in charge of a little life and will play a fundamental role in the formation of their personality and their view of the world. It's overwhelming, but there are numerous sources of education out there that can help you break the cycle of bad parenting. Read trustworthy books about childcare, go to classes, spend time with people who you think are great parents, and learn from them. Never be afraid to ask for help—when something you're doing doesn't feel right, talk to other mothers to find out how they approach the situation.

> ❝ *"I won't ever be able to cover the cost of having a child."*

When you put your mind to it, very little is impossible. With smart thinking, you will be able to save money and get your finances in order.

My first pregnancy came at a time of my life when I lived from paycheck to paycheck. I had no idea how I would be able to dress my baby, afford a car seat, or anything else you need to raise a child. Buying secondhand was a lifesaver. Babies grow out of their clothes pretty fast, and this means anything clothing bought was basically new. You really get a lot of bargains if you know where to look.

Other than that, I suggest you start a savings plan. It doesn't matter if you can only afford to save $10 a month; it is something and will come in handy one day.

> ❝ *"I'm overweight and my body is not in good enough shape to grow a healthy baby."*

It's not only healthy women who get pregnant and give birth to strong, hale and hearty babies. With the help of your doctor, you'll be able to manage any pre-existing health conditions you may have. Furthermore, if your weight is an issue, your pregnancy team will help you with a healthy eating plan, as well as an exercise program. Don't worry, no one will expect you to attend a hard-hitting aerobics class. The exercises will most likely include some light walking and stretching.

Whatever the cause for your concern may be, remember that you have a team of professionals carrying you through your pregnancy, and they will make sure you're giving your baby all it needs to be healthy.

When it comes to mental health, a lot of women may experience some issues during their pregnancy. For many, it will be their first time going through depression. Women who have a history of mental illness, including bipolar affective disorder, chronic depression, and other psychosis, will be more likely to become mentally unbalanced when pregnant.

If you know you struggle with your mental health, open communication with your doctor or midwife is vital. Your doctor will be able to tell you if the medication you're currently on will have to change, how your mental health may change during your pregnancy, and what support you can expect from your pregnancy team.

A lot of women feel embarrassed to tell their doctor or midwife that they're struggling with their mental health. They expect to be judged or even worse, that their baby will be taken away. Of course, these fears are unfounded since doctors aim to make sure mom is in a good headspace to make it through the pregnancy, as well as take care of her newborn after birth.

Treatment for mental illness during pregnancy and after giving birth may include psychotherapy and taking specific medication. Your doctor will work out a care plan that will include how often you should see a therapist and what medication they recommend you take. All this will be included in your medical notes in case you have to switch doctors for some reason or other.

Furthermore, psychiatric inpatient care is also a possibility for mothers who are really struggling with their mental health. If this is necessary after birth, your doctor will place you in a mother and baby unit, so that you don't have to be away from your little one and miss out on any bonding time.

What I want you to take away from this is that there is no reason for you to feel ashamed and there is help out there for you, momma. Grappling with your mental health does not make you a bad mother. If you feel like a failure because you're dealing with depression or severe anxiety, you may as well feel the same when you get the sniffles or a tummy ache—you didn't decide to get any of these ailments and don't have control over them.

## POSTNATAL DEPRESSION

One in 10 women will experience postnatal depression within a year of giving birth. It can even affect the parent who did not grow the little life (National Institute of Mental Health, n.d.).

It is usual for new mothers to feel a little teary and anxious the first week after giving birth as they adjust to their new normal. This is called the "baby blues," and often only lasts for two weeks. If these symptoms persist and get stronger, you're most likely suffering from postnatal depression.

Women who feel fine the weeks right after giving birth but later develop these symptoms (in the first year of motherhood), could have postnatal depression.

Signs that you may be depressed include:

- Persistent low mood or feeling sad all the time.
- Inability to enjoy anything and a loss of interest in things that previously brought you happiness.
- Feeling tired all the time.
- Sleepless nights but feeling sleepy during the day.
- Struggling to bond with your baby.
- Avoiding contact with other people.
- Problems concentrating and finding it difficult to make decisions.
- Alarming thoughts that include self-harm or hurting your baby.

Often, new moms won't even realize they have postnatal depression. It usually develops gradually, and before you know it, you've lost yourself along the way. For this reason, it is important to share any mood fluctuations with your doctor. They are trained to recognize depression and will be able to advise what medication you should take and help you with techniques that can help ease the symptoms. If they feel they don't have the expertise, they will be able to point you in the way of another health professional who will be able to help.

TREATMENT

You may feel very lonely when you suffer from postnatal depression, but don't worry, there are treatments and support, which will have you feeling your usual happy self in no time.

*Help can come in the form of:*

**Self-help:** The mindfulness practices discussed in this book will lift your mood. What you put into your body also plays a vital role in your mental health, believe it or not. In the later chapters, I will walk you through how food impacts not only your physical health but how you're feeling emotionally.

**Psychotherapy:** Your doctor may recommend you speak to a therapist who will be able to arm you with tools to manage your thoughts and feelings. There are various types of therapy, and the method used depends on the psychologist.

**Medication:** When your depression is so severe that self-help and therapy on their own don't help, then your doctor, in conjunction with your psychologist and a psychiatrist, may decide to prescribe an antidepressant. They will make sure to give you medicine that will be safe during pregnancy, as well as while you're breastfeeding.

## WHAT IS THE CAUSE?

Having a baby is a life-changing event, and it takes time for new moms and their partners to adapt to this new way of life. Looking after a baby is stressful and exhausting, and this in and of itself may trigger depression.

There are also other factors which may increase your risk of getting postnatal depression:

- A history of depression or other mental health problems.
- A history of postnatal depression during a previous pregnancy.

- Lacking a support system during pregnancy and after giving birth.
- Relationship stress between you and your partner.
- Recent traumatic events like the death of a loved one.

## CAN POSTNATAL DEPRESSION BE PREVENTED?

There is no scientific proof that there's anything other than maintaining a healthy lifestyle that will prevent postnatal depression. The only real power you have over the situation is if you know you have a history of mental health problems and discuss it with your doctor. If you yourself don't have a history of depression, but your mother or father grappled with it, it is worth mentioning it to your doctor.

Sharing this information with your pregnancy care team will equip them with the knowledge to make the right decisions for you and your baby's health. They may arrange for you to see them regularly for the first few weeks after giving birth just to monitor how you're feeling.

· · ·

### *Postpartum Psychosis*

Postpartum psychosis is much more severe than post-natal depression. It is always treated as a medical emergency since it can quickly escalate to self-harm or abuse of the baby.

You'd be happy to know that postpartum psychosis is very rare—only two in every 1000 women will experience it (Sit et al., 2006). It is more prevalent in women with a history of mental illness, chiefly bipolar disorder. It usually begins soon after childbirth.

Symptoms to look out for include:

- Delusions
- Hallucinations
- Mania
- Depression
- Loss of inhibitions
- Paranoia
- Restlessness
- Confusion
- Behaving out of character

It is advisable to see your doctor immediately if you think you have postpartum psychosis. If your doctor is not available, phone 911 or go to your nearest emergency room.

Your doctors may already have classified you as high risk if you have a history of depression or have bipolar 1 or 2, or schizophrenia. If that is the case, you most likely have a crisis team to contact if you experience any mood changes.

The thing to remember is that you may not know you have postpartum psychosis until it gets significantly worse. For this reason, your partner, family, and friends should know what signs to look out for and take action.

Hospitalization is necessary in most cases. Ideally, you will be placed in a mother and baby unit, but should there not be space available, you may be admitted to the psychiatric ward. Please don't let this scare you; our minds immediately drift to images of mentally unstable people roaming the halls in various states of confusion. It is not like what we've seen in the movies.

Treatment also includes medications. Antidepressants, antipsychotics, and mood stabilizers are most often given to women who have postpartum psychosis. And, as you get better, your doctor may refer you to a therapist to help you navigate your emotions and change how you think and behave.

With the right treatment, it is possible to make a full recovery and have more children. Although you may have another episode, you will be able to recognize it sooner and get the right care to help you recover quickly.

## MEDITATION DURING PREGNANCY

It's no secret that you'll be going through various challenges during and after your pregnancy. Not only will your life drastically change externally, but you'll also have to deal with emotional and physical changes, too. If we just focus on the hormonal transformation, you can expect mood swings, increased appetite, or no appetite at all, nausea, and upset stomach, to name but a few.

I already touched on the benefits of meditation during pregnancy. I will later walk you through nutritional choices, which will alleviate some of the adverse effects on the mind and body. But, let me share with you some meditation techniques. If you're not sure which is best, try them all and do some research—you will find one that is the right fit.

## 7 POPULAR MEDITATIONS TO TRY WHEN YOU'RE PREGNANT

### 1. Vipassana

One of the most ancient meditation techniques in India, Vipassana translates to "special-seeing." This type of meditation aims to help you see things as they really are. This is good if you're fixated on what-ifs. It will anchor you in the moment and make you aware of how you feel—both physically and mentally.

. . .

## 2. Sound Meditation

This technique makes use of prayers or mantras to help you overcome not only anxiety, but any self-doubt you may be feeling. There is power in words, and you can decide if you want to go with a traditional phrase like "om mani padme hum," which is traditionally used in Vipassana meditation. Or you can create your own positive affirmation to recite to yourself. "I breathe in health for myself and my baby" is one example. If you're struggling with negative feelings about yourself, you can try something like, "I am caring and loving and will be a good mommy."

## 3. Deep Breath Meditation

Here, you will focus on your breath and its pattern. This is the ultimate tension-busting technique and is often used to make people fall asleep. It lowers your heart rate and lessens any strain you may be feeling from being pregnant. I enjoyed resting my hand on my baby bump to feel how my tummy moved as I breathed in and out. I always imagined how my gentle breathing was rocking the baby inside to sleep. Focusing on your tummy is also called deep belly meditation.

All you have to do is lie down in a comfortable position and slowly breathe through your nose. On each inhale, hold your breath for a second and then slowly exhale. You'll be surprised how something so simple makes such a huge difference.

## 4. Visualizations

It's all about taking your mind to a place that you associate with calm and tranquility. If it's not a place, an object like a flower, pebble, crystal, or something similar will do just fine. You can even imagine your growing baby! The goal is to focus on the feelings of peace around you.

## 5. Walking Meditation

If your mind is too restless, and other types of meditation cause nothing but frustration, go for a walk. Not only does exercise itself have benefits, but if you concentrate on controlling your breathing, you'll add a meditative aspect to it. Walking meditation is an excellent choice for those of us who fall asleep during other meditations where you have to sit or lie still for an extended period (unless that is your goal, of course).

. . .

## 6. Third Eye Meditation

The space between your eyebrows is called the "third eye." What makes this area special is the pineal gland. Not only does this gland produce serotonin, which helps you feel happy and gives you a sense of overall well-being, the pineal gland also regulates sleeping patterns.

If you feel stressed, close your eyes and focus on your third eye.

## 7. Forced Muscle Meditation

You will need to put aside more time if you want to do this technique. I prefer doing it at night when I'm getting ready to sleep. For one, I'm already flat on my back in bed with nowhere to go afterward, so I can take my time. Since it helps me get a good night's sleep, I always end my day by either doing this meditation or the body scan mentioned earlier in this book.

The idea is to tense your muscles and then relax them slowly. It's best to focus on one group of muscles, for example, the right upper thigh, then the left side. Start at the top of your head and move down, and when you've tensed and relaxed all areas separately, you can tighten your whole body and then release.

There you go! I hope after reading these techniques, you're excited to try one (if not all) of them. If you're too afraid of attempting meditation on your own, there should be various guided meditations or teachers in your area or online. Just do some research and find someone you trust to help you find your feet in your meditation practice.

## IT'S A TEAM EFFORT: WHY A SUPPORTIVE PARTNER IS IMPORTANT

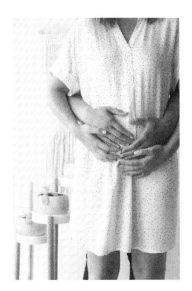

This section is for your partner, so make them a cup of coffee or tea and ask them to read it.

I realize that a lot of mothers may not have a partner —by choice even—and in that case, I want you to know that you can get your support from a best friend or family member, as mentioned earlier. Of course, it will be somewhat different from having a partner in the traditional sense, especially when it comes to the financial aspect of things, but you've got this, no matter what.

To the partners of round-bellied wonders who are growing human beings inside them, your support can have a tremendously positive effect on the health of not only the woman carrying your child, but also on the little one. Science has proven this time and time and again.

One study found that pregnant women who had no support from their partner were more anxious and depressed (Cheng et al., 2016). These researchers felt that partner support was fundamental to a happy and healthy pregnancy.

Another group of scientists came to a similar conclusion but found that financial support also played a role. They found that there was a significant correlation between emotionally and financially supportive partners and the stress levels of soon-to-be mothers (Kashanian et al., 2019).

Your participation in doctor's appointments and pregnancy classes will also decrease your wife's stress levels significantly. This is a good thing, because her health directly impacts that of your unborn child.

You may be thinking, "I want to support her, but I don't know how." Before I share some tips with you on how you can be there for her, the easiest way to know how you can help is by asking.

If you ever feel unsure and you don't know what you can do to make her life a little easier, it never hurts to ask. When you give her an opening to communicate her needs, you will be aware of what exactly you can do during each stage of pregnancy. It may be as simple as running out to the nearest shop to buy chocolate ice cream and gherkins, or maybe something a little more challenging, like reassuring her when she questions her ability to be a mom.

Whatever the case may be, saying "I'm here for you" will already alleviate some of the stress she may be experiencing.

Okay, let's move on to some ways you can up your support game.

## 1. Educate Yourself

As they say, knowledge is power. A lot is happening in your partner's body, and all these changes will affect her mood and how she feels physically. If you know what to expect during pregnancy and after childbirth, you'll be able to better prepare yourself.

Some resources you can use include pregnancy books, childbirth classes, and talking to friends who are new parents and have already been through a lot of what awaits you.

## 2. Communicate

You want your partner to know that she can talk to you about anything. Her mood will fluctuate a lot during pregnancy. One day she may feel confident that she'll make a great mother, the next day she may doubt herself altogether and be consumed by fear. If she has to deal with this turmoil all by herself, she will feel very lonely. Tell your partner that she can share what she's going through with you, and you won't judge her.

## 3. Get Involved

Sometimes, support is as simple as just showing up. Go with her to any medical appointments—it doesn't matter how small. Don't put all the decisions squarely on her shoulders; remember, you're part of the process and should share with her your thoughts and feelings. Also, if she wants to go to a birthing class, ask her when and where—don't make her beg you to go.

*WHAT ABOUT SEX DURING PREGNANCY?*

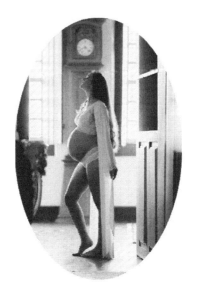

First off, don't feel bad for having questions about having sex with your partner while she's pregnant. Sex during pregnancy is healthy and safe—unless her doctor says otherwise.

There are, however, a few things you will have to take into account.

Not all positions will be comfortable for her. Be patient and gentle as you two work out what feels right for both of you.

There may be times when she is not in the mood for sex. Don't take it personally. Her hormones are on a roller coaster, and this will play a role in her libido. As she gets closer to giving birth, her sex drive may decline altogether. Don't worry, this is common and will get better after the baby's birth.

If you're not sure what she is comfortable doing, ask her. Communication during every aspect of pregnancy is crucial. Use this as an opportunity to talk about sex openly—you can carry it through to life after pregnancy.

I hope this section gave you some insight into why supporting your pregnant partner is vital and how you can be there for her. You may not be the one that has to go through pregnancy, but your role in this tiny being's life cannot be understated. Your responsibility doesn't start once the baby is born, but at the time of that first positive result. By being there for the mom, you're there for the baby. Good luck!

Okay, momma, now that your partner knows how to support you, it's time that you and I talk more about sleep—or the lack thereof.

## SLEEP: WHY IT'S VITAL

We all know what comes after giving birth: late-night feedings, diaper changes, and general sleep deprivation—and tiny hands and feet you can shower with kisses (always remember the good with the bad). But your sleep troubles aren't only going to start after childbirth. That big belly is going to make sleeping difficult, not to mention your tiny bladder, swollen legs, and a myriad of other issues. Don't worry, I have some tips and tricks you can try that will help you get some shut-eye despite these pregnancy ailments.

In the first trimester, you will need significantly more sleep than you're used to. The placenta is growing, and this drains a lot of energy. Don't fight the urge to take a nap in the middle of the day. Your sleep pattern will normalize somewhat in the second trimester. However, that baby bump and other pregnancy-related complaints will start to affect your sleep. This will only get worse in your third trimester, and you'll be able to add back pain, leg cramps, weight gain, heartburn, and a kicking baby to your list of things keeping you awake.

Here are some changes I made which helped me get the rest my body and mind craved so badly when I was pregnant.

1. Minimize or stop drinking fluids a few hours before bedtime. The pressure your baby is putting on your bladder means it is much smaller than usual, so you will get up to go to the toilet an excessive amount unless you limit your fluid intake before bed.

2. Exercise helps improve circulation, and this can help reduce night-time cramps. It also tires one out somewhat, which will make

falling asleep more effortless. That being said, don't exercise two hours before bedtime. The adrenalin that gets released when you're physically active will keep you awake.

3. Clear your head from any worries, to-do lists, and negative thoughts. One way to do this is to write in a diary before turning off the night light. Putting your fears and concerns on paper will resolve some of the anxiety you're feeling, which means better shut-eye.

4. Change your routine to a more soothing and relaxing one. If you're like me, it's a case of washing your face, brushing your teeth, and hopping into bed. But to help you wind down before bed, incorporate some comforting rituals like drinking a cup of warm milk with honey, reading a few pages of an inspirational book, or enjoying a small carbohydrate snack to help release tryptophan, which promotes sleep.

5. As your baby bump grows, you will sleep on your side more often. This can be a very uncomfortable position. When you use pillows under or between your knees and

under your belly, you're one step closer to a good night's sleep. There are special pillows made extra long, specifically for pregnant women. If you can, invest in one of those—it was my best friend during my pregnancy.

6. Eat your main meal of the day earlier to prevent heartburn—no later than two hours before bedtime. If you still struggle with heartburn even when your stomach is empty, prop yourself up on some extra pillows. I find fried foods, as well as spicy or acidic foods, tend to worsen my acid reflux. Avoid any foods that do the same to you.

If you apply the above tips, you most likely won't have much trouble getting to sleep.

# 2

## THOSE WHO GROW TOGETHER, GO TOGETHER

*I* absolutely love this chapter, and I think you will too. Knowing what will happen to your body at all points during your pregnancy is helpful—you'll know what to expect and can prepare accordingly. But understanding what changes your baby goes through as they grow is such an exciting process. I know I was surprised when I read my baby was the size of a honeydew melon at 35 weeks pregnant!

In this chapter, I will walk you through milestones for mommy and baby during each trimester of pregnancy.

## FIRST TRIMESTER

Can you believe there is one lone cell slowly transforming into a bouncing bundle of joy?

When the sperm first enters your egg's outer layer of the fertilized egg—also called a zygote—it will form a barrier to keep other swimmers out. Within hours, the lonely zygote will divide until it goes from one single-cell to 100 cells—imagine a ball of cells that's one-fifth the size of a pinhead.

As this clump of cells continues to change, you can expect to notice some changes of your own. You may suddenly have a heightened sense of smell—unfortunately of the good, the bad, and the terrible. This is a side effect caused by the pregnancy hormones estrogen and human chorionic gonadotropin (hCG).

It is the hCG that will change the negative line to a positive one on your pregnancy test—but only at and after the five-week mark. You may have missed your period and suspect that you're expecting, but taking a home pregnancy test at the wrong time may give you a false negative. If you can't wait to take a second test at a later date, your doctor will be able to do a blood test to find out if your suspicions are correct.

In the first trimester, your baby will steadily be growing, and so will your body's ability to take care of this little being it will have to sustain the next nine months. At week seven, the umbilical cord will make an appearance and join the placenta, which has been and will continue to be your baby's lifeline responsible for providing your baby with nutrients and oxygen, as well as eliminating any waste.

Your baby's hands and feet are yet to grow fingers and toes but, instead, look like little paddles. It's only close to the end of the first trimester when they will change into single digits.

At week 9, you have a medium-sized green olive—that is slowly starting to look more human—in your tummy. The most important of your baby's organs, like the heart, lungs, brain, kidneys, and liver, are beginning to take form. Your baby will also start moving as tiny little muscles begin to develop, but you won't feel any dance moves for another month or two.

As you near the 13-week mark, which is the end of the first trimester, you may get a reprieve from some of the pregnancy symptoms. Firstly, your uterus is the size of a large grapefruit at this time, and it is moving up from the bottom of your pelvis to a more front-and-center spot in your tummy. This means the constant urge to urinate may go away (at least for a while).

If you're lucky, you'll also be saying goodbye to nausea, tender breasts and nipples, extreme fatigue, and food aversion. These symptoms may reappear at a later stage, but a small break from feeling horrible is better than no break. Some unlucky women will experience these ailments throughout their whole pregnancy, without interruption.

## SECOND TRIMESTER

To welcome you to your second trimester, your baby can use their facial muscles to smile at you!

Your little one is the size of a closed fist as you enter week 14, and they're enjoying their new size by working on their movement. Gone are the days of jerky twitches. Your baby now has the grace of a tiny ballet dancer. You regrettably won't be able to feel them kick for weeks to come.

One thing you may feel is a sharp sting down one or both sides of your tummy. It can be very alarming, but don't worry, although it is painful for you, your baby is fine. Doctors call this round ligament pain, and it is caused by uterine growth. The ligaments that support the uterus stretch and pull to accommodate the extra weight, and this causes pain in your lower abdomen. It may be extra pronounced when you get up or turn around too fast, and even when you cough or sneeze. To get some relief, prop your feet up and relax.

Varicose veins are something else you may notice during the second trimester. They're caused by the extra blood your body has been producing, which causes blood vessels to swell. You'll spot them mainly on your legs, but they can develop anywhere in the lower half of your body. There are ways to minimize varicose veins, so if you don't have any yet, consider wearing support stockings and make an effort to get up and walk around throughout the day. Raising your legs may also help. The idea is to keep blood circulating freely. That being said, some women will not be able to prevent these veins—if your mom had them, you'll probably get them, too.

It's during the second trimester that you'll also start to put on some weight. During the first part of your pregnancy, you probably spent a lot of time hugging the toilet and most likely didn't gain a lot of weight. That's all about to change. As your baby gets bigger and bigger, so should you. I say "should" because healthy weight gain during pregnancy is good for the baby, and you don't have the option of taking a "maybe" approach. The ideal is to gain about one pound a week. However, I don't want you to obsess over your weight—if you gain half a pound one week and a little more than a pound the next, it's perfectly fine. The main goal to set your mind on is 4 pounds a month. If you struggle to gain weight or are putting on too many pounds, discuss your diet with your doctor.

At week 16, your baby will be relaxing in your womb while sucking their thumb. How cute is that? What is even more remarkable is that your little one will be able to hear you. The bones in their ears are in place, so go ahead and play them a tune you think they'll enjoy. One study found that babies can recognize songs they heard in utero after they're born (Partanen et al., 2013). You can use this information to your advantage; if they get to know a lullaby while in the safe environment of your tummy, playing them the same song when they're unsettled or upset after birth may have a soothing effect on them. Once you hit the 19-week mark, you may even feel your baby grooving to some music since you'll be able to experience them moving for the first time.

By this time in your preg-
nancy, you may be
wondering if you're having a
boy or a girl. I know you're
itching to decide on a paint
color for the nursery. Well, now is your chance. Week 20 is when you can expect to see external genitals on the ultrasound.

If your baby is a girl, her uterus will be fully formed already, but her vaginal canal is still developing. As if that isn't amazing enough, at 20 weeks, she already has tiny ovaries!

If you're growing a boy, his testicles are still in his abdomen but will descend as soon as his scrotum has finished growing.

On the topic of growing, you may be noticing that your hair and nails are growing more rapidly and are in better condition. This is one of the good things you can thank your pregnancy hormones for—there aren't many others. These hormones increase your circulation, which delivers extra nutrients to cells.

But this is all temporary, and as your hormones drop after pregnancy, so will your hair—literally. Before you imagine bald patches and having to wear wigs, there are ways to minimize your postnatal hair loss! You'll read more about it in the next chapter.

At the 21-week mark, your baby will reach another milestone: taste. Your baby can now swallow some of the amniotic fluid for nutrition and hydration. More than that, they'll be able to taste what you ate. And I have good news—you can start teaching your baby to eat their veggies while they're still in your tum-tum! Research found that babies were particularly fond of the tastes they were exposed to in utero (Mennela et al., 2001). So, eat your veggies now to stop your child from desperately trying to hide peas in their pockets later in life.

Now for something strange—foot growth—and I'm talking about yours, not the baby's! Yes, you read right. At 22 weeks pregnant, you may notice your feet are getting bigger. Pregnancy swelling takes some of the blame for going up a shoe size, but then there's also relaxin, another sometimes pesky pregnancy hormone. Relaxin is responsible for loosening up all the ligaments and joints around your pelvis, but the problem is, this hormone doesn't just focus on the pelvic area. The ligaments in your feet also relax, making it possible for the bones to spread and your shoe size to increase.

Let's look on the bright side; at least now you don't have to make up an excuse to buy new shoes.

But I'm not done yet—the second trimester keeps on giving.

You're 23 weeks pregnant now and not only do you have to deal with growing feet, but you can also expect:

- A fuzzy mind
- Red palms
- Heat rash
- Skin tags
- Stretch marks

But it's all worth it. While you're combatting all these new symptoms, your baby is steadily growing. At week 25, your eggplant-sized tiny one is developing startle reflexes and may even have some locks to show off—albeit not so luscious.

Jumping to week 26, guess who's looking at your insides? Your baby's eyes have been closed to give the retina time to develop, but now they will slowly start to open, and your baby will be able to see what is going on around them. Although, I don't think the view is all that great.

The iris part of the eye doesn't have much pigmentation—it will only fill in over the next month or two. Even if you were able to see the color of your baby's eyes, it might not be permanent. Your baby will keep you guessing for a whole year after birth. The most dramatic eye-color changes will take place when your little one is six months old.

THIRD TRIMESTER

You're getting close to the finish line! The little miracle you're creating weighs around 2 ¼ pounds and is almost 15 inches long in week 28. They're slowly starting to settle into a birthing position—head facing downward. Other than that, you can imagine those tiny eyes blinking as your baby continues to learn the skills necessary for the real world. Coughing, hiccupping, and deeper breathing are only some of the abilities they're working on.

The third trimester will be a busy time for soon-to-be-moms and their partners. There are a few niggling issues you'll have to discuss and some information you'll need to gather.

One of the decisions you'll have to make is to circumcise your baby boy or not. It may not be a topic you paid particular attention to when you first got pregnant, but since you're close to giving birth, you can't put it off any longer. If you have specific religious or cultural traditions to guide you, the process will be much easier. However, when you have no guidance, making a decision may be challenging. I suggest you talk to your doctor and get a list of the pros and cons of circumcision to help you make the best decision for your son.

While you're discussing circumcisions with your doctor, it's also a good time to sort out some other details.

Firstly, do you know your rhesus (Rh) status? If not, then it's time for your doctor to find out. If you happen to be Rh-negative and your baby Rh-positive, then you'll need to get a Rh-immune globulin (Rho-GAM) jab to prevent the development of antibodies.

Next on your list should be finding out what your doctor's view is on episiotomies. This is a surgical cut made in the area between your vagina and your anus before delivery. The aim is to give your baby a bigger space to exit from. This procedure has positive and negative aspects, but what you want your doctor to tell you is that they'll only do an episiotomy when absolutely necessary.

Another item on your to-do list is counting your baby's movement. From the 28-week mark, you should monitor kicks, swishes, rolls, bumps—all your baby's dance moves. Your little one should move at least ten times an hour.

My doctor recommended I count movement twice a day. I would lie down and wait for my baby to wake up. This usually happens as soon as you start to relax, and this pattern will continue after birth. It's as if they can sense the exact moment you're comfortable or getting ready to doze off for a nap!

As soon as I felt a kick, I started counting up until I reached ten, and then I knew everything was A-OK. It's only when there are fewer than ten movements in two hours that you should phone your doctor.

The times when I felt there wasn't enough movement, I would have a snack. The rise in blood sugar usually got the little one moving.

One thing I remember vividly about the third trimester was the sharp, shooting pain down the side of my leg. As your baby turns and settles into position, their head may press against the sciatic nerve. This is not only uncomfortable but very painful. Sciatica is a tingling sensation or numbness starting at your buttocks and moving down the back of one or both your legs. The pain can range from mildly irritating to excruciating. It usually subsides as the baby shifts, but if you're in agony, you can try doing some stretches, soak in a hot bath, or use a heating pad on the area the pain radiates from.

I think it is important at this time to talk about sex and orgasms and how it will affect your baby. Throughout your pregnancy, your libido will fluctuate, and the times when you are in the mood, you may decide to give it a skip out of fear. But I want you to know it is okay to keep enjoying your sex life. You may need to work around that big baby bump, but other than that, sex shouldn't change while you're expecting.

How babies react during sex depends; some may fall asleep thanks to the rhythmic movements, while others may get excited from all the movement. However they react, it doesn't mean they're aware of what is happening. Believe me, don't miss out on getting frisky when you and your partner are in the mood—it won't be as easy to get the time after giving birth.

Okay, back to your to-do-list.

Be sure to include:

- Birth plan
- Nightgown
- Slippers
- Toiletries
- Towel
- Clothes for going home in
- A cute "welcome home" outfit for your little one

Most important of all, make sure you have a rear-facing infant car seat installed before you leave the hospital. You will be breaking the law if you drive your baby home not strapped into a car seat, not to mention how dangerous it is.

I also suggest you ask your doctor to explain the signs to look for when you go into labor. It can be very stressful if the tiniest of cramps triggers a reaction of hopping in the car and going to the hospital. It's great to know what to expect—actually, it's vital to know. Period-like cramps, vaginal bleeding or spotting, a dull but constant backache, diarrhea, a tight feeling in your uterus, and a water break are some of the most common signals that your baby is ready to enter the world.

But long before that happens, I want you to consider writing your unborn baby a love letter. I know you have a lot of hopes and dreams for your baby, so why not share it with them? I know it's a little weird writing to someone who hasn't even been born yet, but if you visualize your little one as they grow up and think about their happiness, you should be able to put pen to paper.

Also, make it about more than your baby's future. Tell them about your pregnancy; the fact that you craved peanut butter and jelly sandwiches with an anchovy center, or how your feet grew a whole shoe size. The options are endless. They will cherish this letter forever. Just imagine them showing their grandchildren the letter their great-grandma wrote and them all laughing about the lengths you went to satisfy your cravings.

Now that we've covered some of the things you have to do in your third trimester, let's get back to the physical changes you can expect, as well as how your baby is getting ready to come greet you.

Starting in week 32, you may experience what is known as Braxton Hicks contractions. This is somewhat like a dress rehearsal. Your pregnancy hormones are slowly beginning to tell your body, "Listen, it's almost time." Your body will react by flexing its muscles...uterine muscles.

This labor dummy-run, strangely enough, is more intense if you've been pregnant before. If this is your first pregnancy, you may not even notice these contractions at all. It starts as a tightening sensation at the top of your uterus that slowly spreads downwards. Usually, they only last for 15 to 30 seconds but can be as long as two minutes.

I imagine you're wondering how you can tell the difference between Braxton Hicks contractions and real labor. The fastest way to distinguish between the two is by changing your position. If you're sitting, get up and walk around. Braxton Hicks contractions will stop as you start to move. Real contractions will also become stronger and more regular overtime.

When you reach 36 weeks, your baby's growth will start slowing to make sure they'll fit through the birth canal. Instead of using nutrients to grow, they will be stored as energy to get through the delivery process.

Not to alarm you, but your baby's head will be close to the same circumference as their chest at the time of birth! So, it's a blessing that the pause button is pressed on further growth until after delivery.

Of course, only your baby knows when exactly delivery will be. The best we can do is guess. Your doctor will first determine how wide your cervix has opened—in other words, how far you're dilated. Your baby will only be able to fit through once your cervix has opened four inches.

Next, your doctor will check your cervical ripeness—or consistency. It will start out firm, much like the tip of your nose, but when you're close to giving birth, the texture will be more like the inside of your cheek.

Effacement is another clue as to when you may go into labor. This has to do with the thickness of your cervix—before you can push your little one out, your cervix will have to be as thin as it can be. In other words, 100 percent effaced.

The position of your uterus and how close to the birth canal your baby is are the last two aspects to factor in. All these processes can happen over weeks, but for some women, it may all take place overnight.

At 39 weeks, your baby is full-term. Congratulations! The little one will weigh around 7 to 8 pounds and will measure 19 to 21 inches from head to toes. Your baby will be ready to enter the world anytime now, although they can decide to stay put up until 42 weeks.

Here are some things to keep in mind during labor.

**Get comfortable:** Giving birth is not a quick process. You may be there for a while, and you're already going to experience a lot of physical distress —do what you can to stay relaxed.

**Ask for what you need:** Your partner won't be able to anticipate your needs. Furthermore, this is most likely a stressful time for them too, considering that they have you and your baby to worry about. If you need something, whether it's a back rub or a damp washcloth, don't be shy to ask.

**Remember your breathing exercises:** If you opted for an unmedicated birth, you might experience real intense contractions—you may not be able to talk through the pain, but you can breathe through it.

**Stay hydrated:** Your care team may offer you water to keep you hydrated—drink it. I know you may not be in the mood because you have only one thing on your mind, and that is to push your baby out, but you'll feel better if you drink fluids. You can ask your doctor to put you on an IV to maintain your hydration levels.

**Walk around:** Between contractions, it will feel good to change positions. Get up and walk around. It will help you stay in the moment, and the movement of your hips as you walk may help your labor along.

This brings me to your baby's last significant milestone when transitioning from the comfort of your womb to the real world: taking their first breath! The air sacs in your baby's lungs haven't been inflated yet, which means they will have to exert a lot of effort during their first breath to expand these tiny pouches.

Once that is done, and the nurses have made sure your baby is healthy, you'll be able to hold your little one in your arms for the first time. Your new arrival will recognize the sound of your voice, but you'll be a big blur until your baby's central vision has developed fully.

When you hold him or her, you'll see they'll instinctively curl up in the fetal positions. Remember, they spent the last nine months in very cramped quarters, and it will take time for them to realize they can spread out. What's more, since this is the only position your newborn is used to, it will comfort them when they're swaddled. The gentle constraint will remind them of the safe and warm space inside you.

To the mommies who are reading this and are in week 41 of pregnancy and fast approaching week 42 —I know you're concerned. I am sure your doctor has shared with you that it is perfectly normal for your baby to enter the world past the due date. You will just need some extra attention during this time.

Your doctor will most likely monitor your baby's health with some no-stress tests like an ultrasound. They may even discuss having an induction with you. Since your baby is officially late, your uterus isn't such a friendly place to be anymore. To jump-start labor, your doctor will apply a topical hormone that will ripen your cervix, or they may break your water, which will get the contractions going.

When your baby finally enters the world—fashionably late, I may add—their skin may be dry, cracked, and peeling. Don't get a fright; it is only temporary. Your baby will also have longer nails and hair, and they'll be more alert. See, there are some upsides to having a latecomer in the family!

It doesn't matter if your baby was early, on time, or late, now is the time to savor all the firsts: first cuddles, feedings, skin-to-skin contact, etc. This is when the bonding process starts with your baby. But remember, it may take some new mommies a little longer to have these feelings of love and attachment. That is okay. We covered the baby blues and post-natal depression in the previous chapter, so you should know that it's nothing to be ashamed of.

# 3

# PREPARATION IS EVERYTHING

When you're pregnant, you want only the best for your baby and will avoid any unnatural substances and surroundings. This is a good thing because a healthy mom equals a healthy baby. Unfortunately, despite your best efforts, you won't be able to escape pregnancy unscathed. At times, you'll think the only way to ease some of these negative symptoms is by resorting to harmful painkillers or other chemicals. In this chapter, I will share with you natural remedies for alleviating some of the more common adverse effects growing a baby will have on your body.

## NAUSEA AND VOMITING

Some pregnant women only feel a little queasy, while for others, nausea lasts the whole day and even interrupts their sleep. It is a typical symptom of being pregnant and may lead to weight loss early on in your pregnancy. It makes sense, really. Who wants to eat while their stomach is unsettled? If you do lose weight because you cannot bring yourself to eat anything, don't be too alarmed. Studies show that women who lost weight at the start of their pregnancy and picked it back up later in their pregnancy (presumably as the nausea subsided) had the same outcome as women who were able to gain a healthy amount of weight (Kapadia et al., 2015).

Here's how to treat nausea and vomiting the natural way:

- Eat smaller portions, more frequently
- Avoid foods that trigger an adverse reaction
- Don't eat fried, spicy, or fatty foods
- Don't drink while eating
- Stay hydrated
- Exercise
- Take your prenatal vitamins at bedtime

- Go for acupressure
- Try aromatherapy (mint, lemon, and orange are only three aromas that may help).

*Natural Remedies*

**Vitamin B6:** It's not entirely clear why this vitamin reduces nausea, but the fact that it does is good enough for me!

**Papaya enzymes:** These help to break down protein and prepare the body for the digestion of food.

**Ginger:** Why and how it works isn't completely understood, but studies have shown that ginger is just as effective as prescription nausea medication—and has fewer side effects (Mohammadbeigi et al., 2011).

**Peppermint:** Calms an upset stomach and alleviates bloating.

**Magnesium:** You'll most likely have a magnesium deficiency when you're pregnant. If you up your intake, your morning sickness may be a thing of the past.

**Citrus fruits:** You may be surprised to learn that citrus actually neutralizes stomach acid, which will settle down an upset tummy.

There are various homeopathic remedies that may help, but please check with your doctor first since some of these substances may be harmful to you and your baby.

## FOOD AVERSIONS AND CRAVINGS

You may find yourself sending your partner out in the middle of the night to buy a bag of Doritos to go with your ice cream. Then again, you may pull your nose up at your favorite snack. Cravings and food aversions are a reality of pregnancy. The problem comes in when you're giving in to your cravings too often and end up putting on too much weight. On the other hand, you may not eat enough because you can't stomach most foods, and your baby won't get all the nutrients they need to grow big and strong.

Common aversions and cravings include meat, eggs, milk, onions, garlic, tea and coffee, and fried food. Of course, this is not an exhaustive list, and it differs from woman to woman. In fact, some women crave non-food substances that may be harmful, such as chalk or dirt. If you experience this, it is usually a sign of an underlying problem, so give your doctor a call.

Other than that, listen to your body. If it wants you to avoid specific foods and craves others, go with the flow. Just make sure you're eating enough nutritious food and not indulging in too many unhealthy cravings.

## HEARTBURN

It's not always what you eat that triggers heartburn—it's yet another symptom of pregnancy hormones. These hormones can make the valve at the end of the esophagus, and the entrance to the stomach, relax, resulting in it not closing correctly. This means acid and the stomach's contents get pushed back up into the esophagus, which causes a burning feeling in your throat and chest. As your belly grows larger, acid reflux will only get worse—your uterus will press on the stomach, which will force the food up through the valve.

Some tips to ease heartburn:

- Avoid foods that make it worse. Fatty, fried, and greasy foods, caffeine, and carbonated drinks are only some examples.
- Eat slowly and chew your food properly.
- Don't drink any liquids during meals.
- Avoid eating two hours before going to bed.
- Don't lay down after eating.
- Sleep on more than one pillow.

*Natural Remedies*

**Apple cider vinegar:** Helps balance your stomach's pH.

**Coconut water:** High in electrolytes, coconut water promotes pH balance throughout your body, which in turn controls acid reflux.

**Lemon water:** Mixing a small amount with water and drinking it has an alkalizing effect. This will neutralize any excess acid in your stomach.

**Yogurt:** Soothes your tummy.

**Fermented foods:** Kombucha, sauerkraut, and other fermented foods are packed with beneficial probiotics that help protect the stomach lining.

**Bentonite clay:** Found in tablets, capsules, and powder form, bentonite clay works wonders if you take it before meals, as it brings down acid levels.

**Aloe Vera:** Purified and decolorized aloe vera juice is effective in reducing acid reflux due to its soothing properties.

**Digestive bitters:** A great way to calm your digestive system.

**Chewing gum:** More saliva is produced when you chew, and this makes you swallow more, which clears the acidity in your mouth and esophagus quickly.

**High enzyme foods:** Eating foods that contain enzymes will speed up the digestion process. Pineapple, papaya, mango, banana, avocado, honey, ginger, and fermented foods all contain digestive enzymes.

**Slippery elm bark:** This has an anti-inflammatory effect on the digestive system. It also has a calming effect and protects against the damaging effects of heartburn on the esophagus. Marshmallow root has similar capabilities.

**Beet kvass:** It increases acid production, which sounds like the exact opposite you want to happen, but a lack of acid can also cause acid reflux.

**Dandelion tea:** Improves digestion.

## CONSTIPATION AND HEMORRHOIDS

Constipation ranks high on the list of annoying pregnancy symptoms, and hemorrhoids are usually a painful side effect.

Three out of four women complain of constipation, bloating, hemorrhoids, and other gastrointestinal discomfort during pregnancy (Johnson et al., 2014). Luckily, these issues can often be prevented by changing your lifestyle.

These slight modifications to your routine will help:

Stay hydrated. If you have enough water in your body, there will be enough fluids to keep your stool soft and make it easier to pass. Also, avoid drinking cold water as this will contract your intestines, and there won't be any movement. Prune juice is a good idea when you're really struggling.

- Eat enough fiber. High-fiber foods like fruit, vegetables, whole grains, and legumes will help regulate your bowel movement. You can talk to your doctor about using a fiber supplement.

- Do something physical every day. If you move, your bowls will move!

- You can also try homeopathic remedies such as Bryonia, Calccabonica, Nux-vomica, etc. but always check with your doctor first.

- Consider going for acupressure to help relax your bowels. Applying pressure to specific points will signal your body to "turn on." It's like flipping a light switch. Think of constipation as an energy blockage, and acupressure is just the push it needs to get moving. You don't have to be a trained acupuncturist to do it; you just have to know which points in your body correspond to which systems. For your digestive tract, you'll want to pinch between your index finger and thumb of your left hand.

- Meditation and relaxation will help to release stress—the tension you feel when

anxiety constricts the whole body,
including your digestive tract.

*Natural Remedies*

**Magnesium citrate:** This mineral regulates the
contraction of all muscles, which means it plays a
role in releasing the bowel.

**Cod liver oil:** Not only is this a champion when it
comes to natural treatments for constipation, but it is
also high in one of the good fats—omega-3 fatty
acids. Omega-3 regulates the release of
prostaglandin, a hormone that ensures the proper
movement of stool. Cod liver oil also reduces inflammation, which is good for intestines that are under
strain.

**Coconut oil:** Has a lubricating effect, stimulates
bowels, and softens stools.

**Pre- and probiotics:** Good gut flora means your
overall system will work better.

**Fermented foods:** Containing beneficial bacteria, yogurt, kefir, kimchi, tempeh, and other
fermented foods ease gastrointestinal discomfort.

**Digestive bitters:** Stimulating the production of saliva, stomach acid, and bile reduces the unpleasant side effects of being constipated.

When it comes to hemorrhoids, the above remedies will work, but you may also want to make sure you don't wait too long before going to the toilet when you feel the urge. If you hold in your stool, the water will get sucked out, and it will be harder to pass, which means you'll have to strain more.

If you have a desk job where you sit for long periods, get up and walk around more often. When you're at home, try to sit on your side to relieve pressure on your rectal veins.

## STRETCH MARKS

I know a lot of women worry about how their belly will look after stretching and then shrinking again. A lot of pregnant women get stretch marks—your tummy grows at such a rapid rate that it's pretty much unavoidable. But, if you keep your skin hydrated by drinking enough water and using topical creams to add moisture, you're less likely to get this type of scarring.

At first, it will appear as a thin red or purple line. The texture around the scar will change as the stretch mark gets older. As time goes by, it will turn translucent and somewhat shiny.

Although stretch marks fade over time, you may not be willing to wait that long. While you will not be able to get rid of stretch marks entirely, since they're a type of scar, some remedies can reduce the appearance. I do suggest you try to keep treatment natural as some beauty products have a lot of dangerous chemicals as ingredients.

Do keep in mind that none of these treatments—chemical or natural—are quick fixes. You will have to commit to a regular skincare routine to see real results.

*Natural Remedies*

**Aloe Vera:** Helps regenerate skin tissue.

**Cocoa butter:** Moisturizes the skin to keep it elastic during stretching.

**Cucumber and lemon juice:** The acidity from the lemon juice will heal the skin, while the cucumber juice provides a soothing effect.

**Apricot:** The exfoliating properties of apricots will remove the top layer of skin and reduce the appearance of stretch marks. Apricot oil also rejuvenates the skin.

**Castor oil:** Provides the moisture and nourishment needed to smooth out stretch marks.

**Vitamin A:** Also referred to as retinoids, vitamin A makes the skin appear smooth and youthful. You will find it in a lot of topical creams. Carrots and sweet potatoes contain a lot of vitamin A. You can also drink an oral supplement.

For some reason, I got more stretch marks during my second pregnancy than my first. This encouraged me to find a miracle ointment to help my new tiger stripes fade—I knew there wasn't a natural way to remove them altogether.

I had remarkable results with a mask made from egg yolks, lemon juice, oatmeal, almond paste, and milk. I would mix these ingredients and lather the mixture over my entire belly every other night. My red lines from my new pregnancy became lighter, and the stretch marks that were already silver from my first pregnancy got smaller.

Here's the recipe:

- 2 egg yolks
- 2 tbsp lemon juice
- 2 tsp oatmeal
- 2 tsp almond paste
- Milk to form a smooth paste

## HAIR LOSS

While you're pregnant, you will have luscious locks, but after giving birth, the drop in hormones won't count in your favor. It's normal for women to lose 100 strands per day. When you're pregnant, it will be significantly less, leading to a fuller head of hair. Fast forward to your postpartum days, and you can expect to lose up to 500 strands a day!

But don't worry, you're not going bald; postpartum hair loss is usually not permanent. To stimulate hair growth and reverse hair loss, you will have to take a multi-prong approach.

Let's look at some lifestyle changes that will help:

- Eat a protein-rich, nutrient-dense diet. Some high-protein foods that contain other pro-hair nutrients include eggs (high in biotin), fermented dairy products (calcium is necessary for healthy hair), and red meat (iron and B vitamins fight hair loss).
- Avoid using tools like hairdryers, curling irons, and straighteners, as well as harsh chemicals that will damage the hair shaft.
- Stretch how long you can go without washing your hair, and don't brush your hair when it is wet as that is when it is most fragile.
- Don't style your hair in ways that will cause damage, including ponytails, buns, braids, and most other up-dos.
- Take care of yourself by getting enough sleep and reducing stress, as both these aspects contribute to hair loss if neglected.

*Natural Remedies*

These ingredients will make a difference when ingested or when used as a treatment on your hair.

**Eggs:** Eggs are high in protein and contain healthy fatty acids that will have a positive impact on your overall scalp health. The vitamin A in eggs will help combat dandruff. If using raw eggs on your hair isn't something you're keen to do, opt for mayonnaise. It has the same fatty acids with the added benefit of moisturizing your hair.

**Castor oil:** Not only rich in fatty acids but also works as an antimicrobial to help put a stop to a flaky scalp, while promoting healthy hair growth. Castor oil should be applied on your scalp and hair, and not consumed as it is very dangerous for your baby in the early stages of pregnancy. It also has a laxative effect.

**Avocado:** A superfood for various reasons. High in protein, fatty acids, and an array of vitamins, avocado will not only hydrate your hair but heal your scalp as well.

**Vitamin E and C:** Both high in antioxidants; will do wonders for your health in general, while promoting hair growth.

**Zinc:** Your hair loss may be exacerbated by a zinc deficiency. Yogurt, cashews, chickpeas, red meat, cheese, and some seafood are good sources of zinc. Alternatively, ask your doctor for a supplement that is safe to use during breast-feeding.

## HIGH BLOOD PRESSURE

You may not have had blood pressure (hypertension) when you got pregnant, but it may develop sometime during. Whether you have chronic hypertension, high blood pressure that was present before pregnancy, or gestational hypertension, the kind that develops around the 20-week pregnant mark, there are things you can do to bring your blood pressure down.

Other than chronic and gestational hypertension, you can also get preeclampsia, where high blood pressure developed after 20 weeks of pregnancy goes together with signs of damage to the kidneys, liver, or brain. If left untreated, it can be fatal for mother and baby.

By taking care of yourself and focusing on your well-being, you'll be able to manage hypertension:

- Don't skip your doctor appointments before and during pregnancy.

- Take your blood pressure medication as prescribed by your doctor.
- Exercise to increase blood circulation and lower blood pressure. If you're sedentary, your chances of developing gestational hypertension are much higher.
- Eat a healthy balanced diet that includes a lot of fresh vegetables and fish (Royal College of Obstetricians & Gynecologists, n.d.). I recommend looking into the Mediterranean diet.
- Limit your salt intake. Although your body needs a small amount of sodium, too much will worsen or lead to hypertension. Use other spices to replace the salt in your diet. In addition, avoid eating processed or fast foods that are packed with sodium, among other unhealthy ingredients.
- As with all pregnancy ailments, limiting your stress will work wonders, especially to manage your blood pressure.
- Don't smoke or consume alcohol. I know this goes without saying, but the fact that these substances push up your blood pressure is even more reason to stop.
- If you're overweight, you will have to pay

extra attention to how much weight you gain. Carrying excess fat puts you at a high risk of hypertension.

*Natural Remedies*

**Bananas:** Getting enough potassium in your diet is very important if you're trying to manage your blood pressure.

**Apple cider vinegar:** Proven to help balance blood pressure, it also has a positive impact on your cholesterol and is considered extremely healthy in general (Kondo et al., 2001).

**Magnesium:** You've seen magnesium mentioned quite a few times as a natural way to help combat pregnancy-related ailments. Pregnant women must get enough magnesium in their diet. Tofu, avocado, banana (two birds with one stone, right), almonds, and soy milk are some foods that are high in magnesium. Eat enough of these to bring down your blood pressure.

## HIGH BLOOD SUGAR

Gestational diabetes affects only 10% of pregnant women in the U.S. each year (Zhu & Zhang, 2016).

This type of diabetes will go away after you give birth, but it can raise your baby's risk of getting type 2 diabetes. You may either get class A1, which you can manage through diet and exercise, or class A2 where you'd need to take insulin and other medications.

Symptoms include excessive thirst, increased appetite, and frequent urination.

To manage class A1 gestational diabetes, you will have to make the following lifestyle changes:

- Change your diet to a low-carb one that doesn't include any sugar.
- Make sure to get moderate exercise for 30 minutes every day.
- Don't gain more weight than is healthy. Your chances of developing gestational diabetes are particularly high when you gain weight too quickly. I'll cover healthy weight gain in the next section.

## WEIGHT GAIN

It is perfectly normal for you to gain weight during your pregnancy. You will, however, have to find a balance between gaining too much or too little weight. If you put on too many pounds, you're at high risk of getting gestational diabetes, hypertension, and experiencing complications during delivery. The chances of you getting those dreaded pregnancy stripes also increase significantly. If you don't gain enough weight, then your baby may be a preemie or born too small, and you may experience childbirth complications.

To keep an eye on your weight, weigh yourself weekly at the same time of the day, wearing the exact same clothes, and using the same scale. Your body fluctuates too much to get on the sale daily—you'll only drive yourself crazy.

It is recommended that a woman with a healthy weight and who gets 30 minutes of moderate exercise takes in a certain amount of calories:

- First trimester: 1,800
- Second trimester: 2,200
- Third trimester: 2,400

Of course, your doctor will be the right person to speak to about how much you need to eat to gain a healthy amount of weight.

Generally speaking, you're looking at gaining 1 to 4.5 pounds in your first trimester, and 1 to 2 pounds per week in your second and third trimesters (American pregnancy associations, n.d.).

The only thing you have to keep in mind is this: if you eat unhealthy food, your baby is also eating unhealthy food. Make sure you eat a well-rounded diet that provides crucial nourishment for your little one. Ditch the takeaways and overly-processed meals.

Since this book is heavily focused on nutrition, you will find out precisely what is and isn't allowed on your plate in the following chapters.

# 4

## HOW TO FUEL A PREGNANT BODY

*A*s you should see by now, a lot is happening in your body while you're making a baby. You will need to adapt your eating habits accordingly. Maybe you're used to following a nutrient-dense, balanced diet—that's great! It will be easier for you to know and understand what your body needs when you're pregnant and why. That being said, as a mom-to-be, you'll have to tweak what you eat to get a vitamin and mineral boost.

For those of you who haven't been following the healthiest of diets and who relied on takeaways, microwave meals, and other processed foods, changing the way you fuel your body may be a little more challenging for you. You only have to remind yourself that a diet based on variety, balance, and moderation plays a key role in keeping you and your little one healthy. When your baby is living in an unhealthy uterine environment, not only may there be difficulties during childbirth, they are at high risk of getting diabetes and heart disease in their adult years. That's not something you'd ever want your child to go through, so let's give them the best possible start.

Let's look a little closer at pregnancy changes and why your body will react to food differently.

The first significant change is your body has to increase its workload—your organs will have to manage doing all the work they did before pregnancy, and on top of that, now have to help develop a baby.

The hormones—estrogen, progesterone, renin, prolactin, hCG, and hPL (human placental lactogen) —cause significant changes to the mother's heart and kidney function, skin, body fat, uterus, and breasts, to name but a few.

The more you know about how your body is changing, the better you'll be able to understand how you can make things easier and take some strain off of your internal workings.

## HEART AND KIDNEY FUNCTION

Your heart will be pumping more blood each minute that it is used to. The hormone erythropoietin—secreted by the kidneys—stimulates red cell formation leading to an increased volume of blood in the body. Furthermore, the hormones estrogen and relaxin will cause the blood vessels to dilate and relax, and this will lower your blood pressure.

Probably the most noticeable change of heart and kidney function will be swollen hands and ankles. The renin-angiotensin system that regulates your body's fluid and electrolyte balance, as well as blood pressure, gets activated and leads to fluid retention. One would imagine that the increased volume of fluid in your body would push up your blood pressure, but the dilation of blood vessels prevents this from happening.

## SKIN

We've covered stretch marks, but you may also notice some light brown blemishes on your skin—usually on your face. This pigmentation is called melasma and is caused by excess pigment-forming cells (melanocytes) in your skin. It's not permanent and will fade away a few months after giving birth.

You may also see small dilated blood vessels on your skin. This is related to the extra high level of estrogen in your body. As with melasma, these blood vessels will go away.

## BREASTS AND UTERUS

Your breasts will increase in size thanks to the hormones estrogen, prolactin, and hPL. This is in preparation for breastfeeding. The only thing stopping lactation while you're pregnant is the high level of progesterone in your body, but you may still notice some fluid discharge from your nipple. This isn't milk, but colostrum.

After you've given birth, levels of certain hormones will dip, and milk production will increase. When the progesterone level is low enough, lactation will occur. During the time that you're breastfeeding, the suckling will stimulate the release of prolactin, which will keep milk production going.

Overall, hCG, hPL, placental growth hormone, estrogen, and progesterone will encourage your baby's growth, help with the transfer of nutrients to the little one, and ensure there is enough blood from the placenta to the fetus (Kumar & Magon, 2012).

## OTHER HORMONAL CHANGES

Your thyroid function will undergo a major change in the first trimester, and your doctor will monitor for any thyroid-related issues. One thing is sure, soon-to-be moms will have to increase their iodine intake during their pregnancy either by adding iodine-rich foods to their diet or through supplementation.

Your body will also go through a period of insulin resistance—usually in the second half of pregnancy. Insulin helps break down glucose (sugar) in your body, and if a balance of insulin and blood sugar levels isn't maintained, gestational diabetes may occur.

As you can see, significant changes take place behind the scenes when you're pregnant. The ones listed above aren't even half of it, but I wanted to give you a basic idea of how every system in your body will function differently, from your brain to your skin. This is why focusing on what you put into your body is so vital.

In the section below, I will break down the macronutrients you'll need during pregnancy, and also cover some other foods, vitamins, minerals you need to pay attention to.

## THE SCIENCE BEHIND FOOD

The food groups you need to eat the most of in your diet are called macronutrients: protein, carbohydrates, and fats. To give you a general idea, a healthy adult would have a macro breakdown of:

- 10-35% protein
- 45-65% carbs
- 20-35% fat

So, this means their daily calories will be divided according to the above. However, that is just a baseline, as a person's macronutrient breakdown is highly subjective. For example, if you decide that you want to follow a low-carb diet, your daily macros would look more like:

- 15-30% protein
- 15-30% carbs
- 40-70% fat

When you're pregnant, your doctor may decide to put you on a low-carb diet, especially if you're already overweight and at high risk of gestational diabetes. Your macronutrients may also change if you're suffering from high blood pressure.

But there's more to it than that—there are bad carbs, fats, and proteins.

. . .

## *Carbohydrates*

The majority of your daily calories will come from carbohydrates, assuming you've not been put on a low-carb diet. Carbs are the primary source of fuel for your body, but not all carbs are created equal.

Refined carbs like pasta, bread, crackers, and basically anything made from white flour, have been stripped of most of their nutrients (but not of their calories). This means if you eat a lot of refined carbohydrates, you'll be missing out on all the good stuff (fiber, vitamins, and minerals). Whole wheat products are better sources of nutrients and contain enough fiber to keep your bowels moving.

On the other side, you do get "enriched" refined grains with iron and folic acid added to the mix, but to me, it makes no sense to remove nutrients during the refining process, only to put them back afterward. It is an unnecessary step which puts food in the processed category, and that's usually not a good thing.

The biggest drawback of refined carbs (this includes cookies, cakes, pastries, etc.) is the blood sugar spike you get soon after eating it. These types of carbs digest very fast, causing a sudden release of insulin and a glucose spike, followed by a crash—feeling sluggish and usually, hungry again. As you can imagine, this isn't good when you're pregnant. Not only does it put you at risk of getting gestational diabetes, but it's also just not nice to feel tired on top of the tiredness you're already feeling!

Complex carbs—the type you get from veggies and whole grains—take longer to digest.

I suppose it's all about how extreme you want to get. Some women prefer to eat foods in their most natural form, while others don't mind indulging in pasta, cereals, bagels, and other processed and refined carbohydrates. The best advice I can give is to listen to your body; if you don't feel at your best eating the way you do now, make a change.

### Fats

When it comes to fats, things get even more confusing. Eating enough "good" fat and limiting "bad" fat is essential for good health. There are some fats that are extra important during pregnancy as they aid your baby's brain and eye development—not only in utero but long after birth (Phang et al., 2020).

But what fats are considered good?

There are four kinds of fat: monounsaturated, polyunsaturated, saturated, and trans fat. However, it's not as clear cut as that—fats usually don't fall into only one of these categories. Take palm oil as an example. It is made up of roughly half monounsaturated fat, half saturated fat, and some polyunsaturated fat, too.

Monounsaturated and polyunsaturated fats are considered good. These fats also contain vitamin E, which is high in antioxidants—super helpful to your body during pregnancy.

Olives, avocados, nuts, peanut oils, and nut butters are good sources of monounsaturated fats. Interestingly enough, monounsaturated fats can actually lower your cholesterol (Cleveland Clinic, n.d.). This is not something you'd expect to hear considering how we've been led to believe that all fat is bad.

Polyunsaturated fats are also good for you; they contain omega-3 fatty acids such as DHA and ALA, both of which are vital in your baby's brain and eye development. Flaxseed, walnuts, soybean oil, and cold-water fish are only some of the sources high in polyunsaturated fats. Since your body doesn't make essential fatty acids, they should always be included in your diet.

When it comes to the "bad bin," saturated and trans fats should be avoided. High-fat meat and whole milk are two sources of saturated fat you can easily limit in your diet. When it comes to trans fats, you will find it in most packaged foods as it extends the shelf life. For this reason, crackers, chips, cookies, and any other processed foods should be avoided.

This reminds me of a tip I always give my clients when they come to me for nutrition advice: always stick to the outer edge of the grocery store. They usually pack all the fresh and healthy foods there, while the processed foods with questionable ingredients are generally in the center.

Okay, back to fat. The bottom line is, fat is a critical component of a healthy diet for various reasons. For one, your body cannot absorb vitamins A, D, E, and K that are particularly crucial during pregnancy without fat to facilitate the process.

. . .

## *Protein*

Protein is the building block of all muscle and body tissue. Eating enough protein is particularly important during the second and third trimesters when your baby is doing most of their growth. It is recommended that pregnant women eat up to 2.46 ounces of protein every day. Of course, this is bearing in mind your current weight and activity level.

One study found that protein consumption is considerably more crucial than carb intake. Eating a high-carb diet actually suppresses placental growth, which means your baby will be born below a healthy weight (Clapp, 2002). This, in turn, can lead to cardiovascular issues later in your child's life.

Protein also contains amino acids that control key metabolic pathways of your baby's growth, development, neurological functioning, immunity, and overall health. During pregnancy, your amino acid levels will decrease noticeably, and you will have to pay extra attention to eating enough protein. If you do not have enough amino acids in your body, it may lead to congenital malformations. In fact, amino acids are so crucial, your doctor may test your levels throughout pregnancy to ensure you're within healthy limits.

If you follow a vegetarian diet, you'll have to pay extra attention to making sure you meet your daily protein needs. Beans, yogurt, eggs, milk, and soy products are excellent protein sources for vegetarians.

For the meat-eaters, lean meats, fish, and poultry are perfect for boosting your protein intake. You can also add beans, lentils, dairy, nuts, and soy products to your diet.

That covers the macronutrients, but there are some other ingredients to the perfect pregnancy diet that is worth mentioning.

**Tissue salts:** You're building an entirely new human from a single cell, and cell salts, or biochemic salts, are necessary for the healthy development of your baby. They will also help you maintain your own mineral reserves. Without these mineral builders, basic functions such as absorbing food, water, and oxygen can't happen. These salts are found in rocks, soil, plants, and animals. It is best to talk with your doctor to find the correct dose.

**Folic acid**: This is a B vitamin that will help your baby grow. It reduces the risk of spina bifida and other neural tube (brain and spinal cord) defects. Citrus fruits and juice have a high folic acid content, but you can also find it in enriched bread, flour, pasta, cereals, and other grain products. The daily recommended dose of folic acid for healthy women who aren't pregnant is 400 mcg. During pregnancy and while breastfeeding, you should aim for 600 mcg per day. You will need to take an oral supplement during this time since it will be tough to get this amount from foods alone.

**Vitamin C:** Supplementing vitamin C will reduce the risk of preeclampsia (sudden increase in blood pressure), intrauterine growth restriction, and other pregnancy complications. It will also help you fight anemia.

**Iron:** As the amount of blood in your body increases when you're pregnant, you will need more iron for yourself and your baby. Iron plays an essential role in your little one's brain development, so you should make sure to get 27 mg of iron a day.

**Calcium:** Not only does calcium build your baby's bones and teeth, it also reduces your risk of preeclampsia. A dose of 1,000 mg per day is recommended.

**Vitamin D:** You will need to up your vitamin D intake to ensure that the calcium you're taking is absorbed. Pregnant or not, 600 IU (international units) is necessary for optimal results.

# 5

# THE PERFECT MENU

*A* lot of soon-to-be mommies suffer from nutrient deficiency as the body exerts itself to make a whole new human. Your baby will need a lot of the vitamins and minerals you yourself need to feel great. Fortunately, you can make up for all the things your baby steals from you by putting extra emphasis on eating healthily and supplementing where you know you may have deficiencies.

Before I move onto foods that are good for mom and baby alike, let's first debunk some old wive's tales.

## PREGNANCY MYTHS BUSTED

Millions of words have been written about pregnancy and what to eat to feel more energized and to support your infant's growth. Unfortunately, a lot of the information out there is based on  the ways our mothers' mothers did things and aren't based on scientific fact. Let's look at some of these myths.

### *1. You should eat for two.*

I'm sure you've heard that saying more than once. And yes, you will technically be eating for two, but that doesn't mean you should double up your portions. It's more about what you're eating than how much you're eating. Gaining unnecessary weight will make childbirth more challenging and may increase your need to have a Caesarean section. You're also more likely to experience vaginal tears and excess bleeding during delivery if you're overweight. But even more significant is the impact excessive pregnancy weight gain will have on your child—it may contribute to your child's risk of being obese (Nicholas et al., 2015).

## 2. Some foods cause miscarriage.

Papaya, pineapple, and green bananas are said to lead to miscarriage. However, there is no scientific proof of this; nor are there any documented cases of miscarriage due to consuming these foods. If you eat a well-balanced diet that contains all your macronutrients, then your baby will be healthy. You can always check with your doctor if you're worried about the effect specific foods will have on your little one.

## 3. Herbs and tonics will give your baby a boost in the intelligence department.

Don't fall for gimmicks and marketing tricks. You will see a lot of teas, tonics, and herbal juju that claim to do this and that for mom or baby. Before buying it, do two things. First, research it and see if these claims are valid. Then when you're sure it will benefit you or your little one in some way, contact your doctor to find out if it is safe.

Most of the time, you will see that no medical or scientific evidence supports these miraculous claims.

## *4. Full-cream milk is better.*

A lot of people will recommend that you drink full-cream milk instead of low-fat/skimmed milk because it contains more nutrients. This is not true. Low-fat and skim milk products have just as much nutritional value as full-cream products and are often the better choice considering that they contain significantly fewer calories.

Now that we got that out of the way, it is time to delve a little deeper into foods and beverages you should include on your menu.

### HEALTHY CHOICES FOR MOM TO MAKE

I've already covered the importance of protein, fat, and carbohydrates. In this section, we'll have a closer look at specific foods that will take your pregnancy diet to the next level.

### *Almonds*

Before you reach for some chips or pretzels, grab a handful of almonds instead. These nuts are full of fiber, protein, and good fats. What makes almonds (and all nuts) idea during pregnancy is that they will keep those hunger pangs at bay. The high-fat content of nuts makes you feel satiated for longer. What's more, just a quarter cup of almonds contains more than a third of your daily vitamin E requirements. If you don't recall, vitamin E is vital for your baby's brain development.

## Avocado

When it comes to a list of superfoods, this fruit is in the top five. Avocados are buttery and rich thanks to the amount of monounsaturated fatty acids they contain. You'll also get a good dose of fiber, B vitamins (especially folate), vitamin E, C and K, potassium, and copper. Packed with so much goodness, avocados are a great choice not only during pregnancy, but always.

The healthy fats in avocado will help build your baby's skin and brain, and the folate will combat any neural tube defects. Since avocados contain potassium, you'll have fewer leg cramps, although bananas should still be your go-to fruit to combat those pesky cramps.

· · ·

### *Broccoli and Dark Leafy Greens*

Vegetables are good for you; there's no doubt about it. But dark green leafy greens are the heroes of the vegetable world. They contain all the nutrients you and your baby will need and usually at a fraction of the price (calories) than other vegetables. They're high in fiber, vitamin C, K, A, calcium, iron, folate, and potassium. Adding a serving of green veggies to your meal is an excellent way to keep your bowels regular.

The health benefits of this bonanza of green goodness doesn't stop there. Leafy green veggies also reduce the risk of low birth weight (Gete et al., 2020).

### *Bananas*

I briefly touched on the high amount of potassium found in bananas. We know that potassium is good for leg cramps, but it also has the ability to regulate your blood pressure and may help lower your risk of preeclampsia. Eating one large banana will mean you've met close to 15 percent of your daily potassium requirements.

Furthermore, the positive effect potassium has on your blood pressure during pregnancy could continue to benefit you years down the road. Research suggests that keeping your blood pressure within a healthy range during pregnancy could prevent hypertension and metabolic syndrome up to 10 years later (Rice et al., 2016).

Wait, let me go get a banana—why don't you join me? Your body would want you to!

## *Berries*

If you ever want proof that dynamite comes in small packages, find some berries. They're jam-packed full of vitamin C, fiber, and super rich in antioxidants.

When following a low-carb diet, berries will be your go-to fruit because they have a relatively low glycemic index, which means they won't cause blood sugar spikes as some other fruits do. Also, berries contain relatively few calories, which is surprising if you consider how good they taste.

## *Dried Fruit*

I see dried fruit as nature's candy. But, just like regular candy, overeating dried fruit isn't recommended. It's high in calories and will lead to weight gain if not eaten in moderation. Apart from hitting just the right spot when you're craving something sweet, dried fruit comes packed with potassium, iron, folate, and fiber. You'll get the exact same amount of nutrients as you'd get eating fresh fruit, but in a smaller form.

Dried prunes are particularly helpful during pregnancy when you're struggling with constipation.

## *Dairy*

You already know that you need to consume extra protein and calcium when pregnant. Milk, cheese, and yogurt are some of the dairy products that can help you achieve your goal. Calcium is probably the first thing that pops into your mind when you think of dairy, and you may be surprised that it also contains a good dose of protein—casein and whey. So, you can tick two essential ingredients of the pregnancy diet off the list after enjoying a glass of milk and some cheese.

Dairy also provides high amounts of magnesium, phosphorus, zinc, and B vitamins. Yogurt is especially beneficial because it not only contains more calcium than other dairy products, it also contains probiotics that will keep your gut happy.

## Eggs

Eggs contain a little of almost every nutrient you need and aren't that high in calories. What makes eggs extra beneficial during pregnancy is the choline content. This vital nutrient is good for your baby's brain and will help prevent any brain and spine abnormalities.

A pregnant woman's recommended choline intake is 450mg per day—one egg contains approximately 147mg.

## Fish Liver Oil

Fish liver oil is rich in all the omega-3 fatty acids your little one needs for brain and eye development. It's also high in vitamin D, one vitamin most of us are deficient in and don't even know it (Nair & Maseeh, 2012).

Fish liver oil is so potent, one tablespoon of it will provide you with more than the recommended daily intake of omega-3, vitamin A, and vitamin D. Due to fish liver oil's high vitamin A content, you should not consume more than one serving a day (15ml). Too much omega-3 may also thin your blood.

## Legumes

Lentils, chickpeas, soybeans, peas, beans, and peanuts all fall under legumes. They're all great sources of fiber, protein, folate, calcium, and iron—all the things your body needs more of when it's building a baby.

Folate is probably the standout ingredient of legumes. One of the B vitamins, folate (B6), is essential for your baby's health, especially during the first trimester. If you can start to supplement with it before pregnancy, even better.

You should get at least 600mcg of folate every day. This number is going to be challenging to achieve without supplementation, but if you add legumes to the mix, you'll be one step closer.

## Seafood

Seafood is one of the areas where you have to pay particular attention to how much and what type of seafood you're eating. Large, predatory fish such as various sharks, swordfish, tilefish, and king mackerel have high mercury content, and that is a bad thing when you're pregnant. If you overeat fish high in mercury, it will build up in your bloodstream and could possibly impair the development of your little one's brain and nervous system.

Now that you know what seafood not to eat and to keep an eye on how much mercury you consume, let's look at what you may eat.

Seafood, in general, is high in protein, iron, zinc, and omega-3 fatty acids. You will by now know that all those nutrients are crucial for your baby's growth.

If you're not sure what fish is safe to eat, always go for salmon. It's low in mercury, high in omega-3s, and has a slew of other health benefits.

Here are some more safe seafood choices:

- Sardines
- Anchovies
- Freshwater trout
- Herring
- Pacific mackerel
- Shrimp
- Pollock
- Cod

- Canned tuna (light)
- Tilapia

## *Water*

Yes, I know adding water to this list is a little out of the blue, but staying hydrated is so important that it definitely belongs with all the other healthy choices you can make.

You read earlier that the amount of blood in your body increases during pregnancy, and your need for water increases as your blood volume does. When you're expecting, you'll typically need 10 ounces of water more per day than you're used to. However, don't stop there. If you're thirsty, drink until you feel hydrated.

When you're dehydrated, you'll suffer from headaches, feel tired, be in a bad mood, and feel anxious. What's worse, it will most likely lead to constipation and urinary tract infections.

Do keep in mind that you also get water from fruits and veggies, and other fluids you consume during the day.

## AN ORGANIC RAINBOW

It's not news that fruits and vegetables are full of vitamins and minerals. We also know that they're good sources of fiber. In the previous section, I talked about the benefits of specifically green vegetables, but I don't want you to think your plate should be limited to the color green.

In fact, you should aim for a rainbow-colored array of fruits and veggies—with the skins intact where possible. You see, fruit and vegetables contain phytonutrients—chemical compounds that contribute to your overall well-being. A lot of these phytonutrients are located in the skins, the parts we usually throw away. Fruits and veggies are also high in antioxidants, which will fight any free radicals.

So, aim for a vibrant-looking plate—the more colors on your plate, the higher the variety of good stuff you'll be eating.

But, will store-bought produce do or is organic better? Well, I'm a firm believer in keeping things as natural as possible, and

nothing is more natural than buying carrots from a local organic farmer.

The problem with fresh produce bought from your nearest grocery store is that they're sprayed with pesticides, weed killers, chemical fertilizers, and some are even genetically modified. I'm not suggesting that organic fruits and vegetables are completely pesticide-free, but organic farmers use far less, which makes it the superior choice. And it's not only fruits and veggies that get blasted with harmful chemicals; mass-produced meat contains hormones and antibiotics!

One study found that pregnant women who ate organic foods were 58% less likely to give birth to a boy with hypospadias—a urogenital birth defect (Brantsaeter et al., 2016). Eating an organic diet also prevents ingesting antibiotics injected into livestock. Consuming these antibiotics may lead to future resistance to those specific antibiotics, which will make treating certain bacteria complicated. Furthermore, organic foods contain no artificial flavors, colors, or preservatives.

Now, I realize that not everyone has the means to buy organic food—prices tend to be a little higher due to the small scale of the operation—or live close to an organic market. If you can't go the organic route, please don't feel that you're somehow less of a mother. We can all only do what we can. And, although eating mass-produced foodstuffs may increase your baby's risk for some diseases, the percentages are marginal. Furthermore, the advantages of eating organic during pregnancy can be mimicked by eating a wholesome, mainly plant-based diet. It has more to do with following a healthy diet than an organic one.

I am going to say that an organic diet is the best choice during pregnancy, only because consuming anything artificial when you're pregnant is a no-no in my books. That being said, it is not the end of the world when you only have access to store-bought produce. As long as you stick to a nutrient dense diet and do everything else in your power to ensure you and your baby are healthy, the adverse effects of any chemicals or antibiotics should be minor.

## FOODS NOT ON THE MENU

Some foods may be okay to eat when you don't have a little bundle of joy growing inside of you, but for the health of you and your baby, it should be left off your plate during pregnancy. Then you'll also find some foods that are allowed in limited quantities. There are scientific reasons why you should avoid or limit certain foods, and I suggest you pay extra mind to this section.

### *Artificial Sweeteners*

What a hot topic! The jury is still out on how safe artificial sweeteners are in general, nevermind when you're pregnant. That being said, most doctors agree that you can use aspartame and sucralose during pregnancy. Of course, I am more in favor of using natural sweeteners like agave, date sugar, honey, or molasses.

However, a 2020 study found that both camps may be wrong: low-calorie, artificial sweeteners, and natural stevia may be good for you, but that doesn't mean they're safe for your baby. The offspring of women who use low-calorie sweeteners during pregnancy and while breastfeeding may struggle with their weight as they grow (University of Calgary, 2020). In addition, non-nutritive sweeteners play havoc on your gut microbes, which means your overall health will suffer, and you'll be more prone to heart disease.

I don't know about you, but I think drinking bitter tea or coffee is a small price to pay for a hale and hearty baby.

## *Caffeine*

Drinking too much caffeine during your pregnancy increases the risk of your baby weighing less than they should at birth. This may open your child up to various health problems later in life. It is recommended that you drink no more than two cups of instant coffee a day. Your total caffeine intake should not be more than 200mg a day.

## *Empty-Calorie Foods*

When you're expecting, it is easy to use cravings as an excuse to overindulge in sugary foods like candy bars, cookies, cakes, soft drinks, candy, etc. There's nothing wrong with treating yourself to a scoop or two of ice cream now and again, but when you start eating too many empty calories, it's a different story.

These types of food not only will make you pack on the pounds, but they are also high in trans fats, which are the absolute worst of the bad fats. Besides that, most empty-calorie, packaged foods are simple carbs, which means your blood sugar and insulin will go on a roller coaster ride after eating that box of cookies.

### *Fish*

I covered the dangers of fish high in mercury in the previous section, but here is a list of what mercury can do to mom and baby.

**Mom:** It can damage your lungs, kidneys, and nervous system. Mercury poisoning also impacts your hearing and vision. The seriousness of the damage depends on the level of mercury you were exposed to.

**Baby:** If your little one is exposed to a high level of mercury while in the womb, the chances of them getting brain damage and developing hearing and vision problems are high.

Shark, swordfish, tilefish, and king mackerel contain too much mercury for you to consume during your pregnancy.

. . .

## Paté

It doesn't matter if the paté is made from meat, fish, or vegetables—it's not safe to eat. When you're expecting a baby, your immune system may not be as strong as it should be due to all the changes taking place in your body. During this time, you are at an increased risk of foodborne illnesses. Paté may contain *Listeria* bacteria, and what makes this type of bacteria extra scary is the fact that you may not show any symptoms, but your baby will be infected.

## Raw Meat

There's a high risk of *Toxoplasmosis* infection if you eat raw meat. As a side note, this bacteria is also present in cat feces, and you should take extra hygiene measures if you own a cat as a pet.

## Raw Eggs

Any foods made with raw egg, for example, mousses or mayonnaise, should be avoided. Also, make sure to cook your eggs thoroughly to kill off any *Salmonella* and other bacteria.

## Refined Carbohydrates

If you recall, we had a look at the difference between refined (simple) carbs and complex carbs in Chapter 4. A quick refresher: refined carbohydrates don't contain all the vitamins, minerals, and fiber their unprocessed counterparts do. They do, however, provide the same amount of calories. But what is more concerning for your and your baby's health is the fact that refined carbohydrates are digested quickly, and this leads to a blood sugar spike. The constant rush of insulin increases your risk of getting gestational diabetes.

### Soft Cheese

Brie, Camembert, and any other mold-ripened soft cheeses aren't recommended in a pregnancy-friendly diet. There is a significant chance that these types of cheeses will contain *Listeria*.

### Sugar

Sugar should not be on the menu for similar reasons as empty-calorie foods and refined carbohydrates. The recommended allowance of free sugars (not from fruits and natural sources) a day is 30g for soon-to-be moms. That translates to seven sugar cubes. To give you an idea of how easy it is to overshoot 30g, one can of cola contains nine sugar cubes.

## Soy

Although you're allowed to consume soy products, you should keep in mind that they may prevent the absorption of calcium, magnesium, copper, iron, and zinc—all the minerals you desperately need while pregnant. It is the phytic acid in soy that is the main culprit that makes it dangerous in large quantities.

Besides that, soy also contains "anti-nutrients" that may interfere with the digestive enzymes in your body.

## Unpasteurized Food

The pasteurization process kills harmful bacteria; without it, you may be consuming bacteria such as *Campylobacter*, *E.coli*, *Listeria*, and *Salmonella*.

## Unwashed Vegetables

First off, fresh produce you bought at your nearest grocery store has been sprayed with a list of chemicals as long as your arm. You have to rinse your fruits and vegetables before you eat them to remove any residue of these harmful substances. Then, there's the issue of bacteria like *Listeria* and *Toxoplasma Gondii,* which may be present on the produce—another reason why giving your fruits and veggies a rinse before eating is a top-notch idea.

### Vegetable Oil

The omega-6 fatty acids in vegetable oil, chiefly linoleic acid, may cause inflammation in your body.

### Alcohol

It's good to keep in mind that what you eat and drink gets passed on to your baby through the umbilical cord. Alcohol is a poison—it doesn't matter how you look at it. So, why would you want to give your little one something so terrible to drink? If you think about how alcohol can lead to miscarriage, stillbirth, and a range of other fetal alcohol spectrum disorders, it's just not worth it.

# 6

# HOW TO COMPLEMENT YOUR DIET

*I*t's challenging to juggle all the vitamins and minerals your body needs when you're pregnant; will you meet your daily requirements through your everyday diet, or do you have to supplement?

Although we touched on some of these vital nutrients throughout the book, this chapter is a cohesive list you can turn to when you're unsure. Of course, as always, discuss any supplements you plan on taking to help your body with your doctor.

## PRENATAL VITAMINS

A healthy diet is the first choice when it comes to getting the vitamins and minerals your body needs. But, as we established, that won't always be possible. Prenatal vitamins will fill the gaps. When you look at which brand is best for you, make sure it contains folic acid, iron, calcium, vitamin D, and vitamins C, A, B, and E, as well as zinc and iodine. Also, if you're not eating enough fish and good fats, you must take omega-3s.

Your doctor may recommend supplementing with higher doses of certain nutrients.

It's time for a closer look at the vitamins and minerals.

### *Vitamin D*

It's not unusual for pregnant women to have a vitamin D deficiency, which increases their risk of gestational diabetes, preterm birth, and preeclampsia. Vitamin D, together with calcium, helps your baby's bones and teeth grow strong. Although your body produces vitamin D when out in the sunlight, you won't reach the recommended 600 IU and will have to get the rest through food and supplementation. Most prenatal vitamins contain 400 IU. The rest you can get by eating salmon, egg, and drinking vitamin-D fortified milk.

## Omega-3 Fatty Acids

Prenatal vitamins usually do not contain omega-3 fatty acids, and you will have to buy a separate supplement if you're not reaching your goal of 200-300mg a day through your diet. Increasing your intake of EPA and DHA may prevent preemies and lowers your risk of preeclampsia, not to mention the role it plays in your baby's brain development, as we discussed earlier. When you have an omega-3 deficiency, you'll be more prone to depression.

## Probiotics

Your gut health is vital during pregnancy. Not a lot of people realize how big of a role gut microbes play in various bodily functions. It's not just limited to digestion. For example, research shows a link between probiotic intake in early pregnancy and a lower risk of premature birth (BMJ, n.d.). If that isn't enough to convince you to start drinking probiotics, there are signs that it may reduce anxiety and depression while you're pregnant (Browne et al., 2019).

## Magnesium

The role of this mineral on various bodily functions has been established throughout *Table for Two*. It stops cramps, helps with constipation, promotes sleep...the list of what it does for the mommy is very long. When it comes to its benefits for your baby, it plays a vital role in preventing preterm weight and decreases the probability of various pregnancy complications occurring. Pregnant women should consume 310mg per day. Keep in mind that all the hormonal changes during pregnancy will cause more magnesium to be excreted in the urine, so you will have to compensate.

## Calcium

Another set of bones will be forming in your tummy, and this makes calcium a crucial nutrient during pregnancy. But calcium won't just play a role in the building of your baby's skeleton; it's also good for your little one's muscles, including the heart, nerves, and hormones. The recommended daily dose is 1,000mg. If you do supplement with calcium, keep in mind that calcium interferes with iron absorption. Never take more than 250mg of calcium with iron.

## Iron

Iron-deficiency anemia is prevalent among pregnant women due to the extra blood that is needed for growing babies. Iron also carries oxygen from your lungs to other parts of your body and your baby, too. It's possible for you to get very close to your daily iron needs by filling your plate with leafy green veggies and other iron-rich foods. Most prenatal vitamins do, however, include iron. You need 27mg a day for your body to produce extra blood.

## Vitamin C

This water-soluble vitamin helps to develop your baby's bones and teeth. For you, it will reduce your risk of cardiovascular disease, repair your tissue, boost your immune system, help your body produce collagen, and best yet, increase your body's ability to absorb iron. It's a powerful antioxidant that everyone should take, whether pregnant or not. It would be best if you tried to eat three servings of vitamin C-rich foods per day. The goal is to get 85mg of this vitamin daily—not a difficult task if you consider that a 6-ounce glass of orange juice and one cup of strawberries will provide you with more than double that amount.

## Folic Acid

If you can start to supplement with folic acid before getting pregnant, you're setting you and your little one up for a healthy pregnancy. It is especially crucial for the development of your baby's neural tube and ensuring it closes properly to form the brain and spinal cord. Folic acid also helps your baby's heart to develop. It's recommended that pregnant women consume no less than 400mcg a day, but ideally, it should be closer to 600mcg.

## Collagen

You may want to supplement with collagen to support your skin, cartilage, joints, blood vessels, organs, hair, and nails. You will, however, have to look for peptide collagen and not marine collagen.

## Vitamin A

This is one of the vitamins you should not supplement with unless explicitly told so by a medical professional. You will meet most of your vitamin A requirements through eating a balanced diet. And, although your prenatal vitamins may contain vitamin A, it will be a safe amount. You should never take more than 4,000 IU a day—anything over 10,000 IU will be toxic.

When it comes to dietary supplements, always look for a seal of approval from trusted organizations such as the United States Pharmacopeia (USFP), NSF International, and Consumer Lab. This way, you can rest assured that your supplements are up to standard and meet rigorous criteria that prove they are safe to use during pregnancy.

## ROUTINE TESTS DURING PREGNANCY

At different times during your pregnancy, your doctor may do some routine tests to see that you and your baby are in optimal health.

These tests include:

**Blood pressure checks:** Your first blood pressure test results will be used as a baseline throughout your pregnancy. This way, your doctor will be able to see if future readings are too high or low. If it is higher than usual, it can be a warning sign of preeclampsia.

**Urine tests:** Your doctor will screen your urine at various times during your pregnancy to check for infections, gestational diabetes, and even preeclampsia. Your doctor may also check for ketones in your urine—if they're present, it may indicate that your diet needs to be adapted to include more carbohydrates.

**Blood tests:** You most likely will only have to undergo blood tests twice during your pregnancy. The first time will be early in the pregnancy when your doctor will determine your blood group, check for infections such as hepatitis B, HIV, or syphilis, find out if you're anemic, or have other blood conditions. Roundabout the 28-week mark, your doctor may recommend a second blood test to check your iron levels, and it is at this time when you'll also get tested for gestational diabetes if you show any signs. Other reasons why you may have to go through additional blood tests are to check your Vitamin D levels, as well as thyroid function.

# 7

# MAINTAINING POSTPARTUM HEALTH

*Y*ou made it through nausea, backaches, swollen feet, sleepless nights, and all the other unpleasant pregnancy-related ailments. But wasn't it worth it to be able to look at your newborn's little face and hold their tiny body in your arms?

The following few months aren't going to be much easier, and you will have to face different challenges as you and your baby bond and find a rhythm to your days. You must continue to look after your health by continuing to follow a wholesome diet. I know you may feel too tired to prepare a healthy meal, and the idea of visiting a drive-through or buying a quick and easy processed meal will look much more appealing. Don't do it!

Remember that what you are putting in your body will still transfer to your baby when you are breastfeeding. Nevertheless, if, for some reason, you can't or decide against breast milk as your newborn's source of sustenance, healthy eating will make other aspects of being a new mom more manageable.

If you're not sure what to expect after giving birth, this chapter will share with you all the information and equip you with tools to transition back to your pre-pregnancy body.

## POSTPARTUM REPLETION

Pregnancy took a toll on your body, and it's not over yet—now it's time to breastfeed your baby. This will be a difficult time for your body if you add the limited sleep to the mix. You'll feel like your brain isn't working like it used to and wonder if your ability to focus will ever come back. You'll have no energy and will feel like your body hasn't been the same since getting pregnant and giving birth. The only way to manage this time in your life is by fuelling your body with nutrient-dense foods that will provide you with a much-needed energy boost while ensuring your baby is getting all they need for optimal development.

You have to make conscious decisions to replenish all the nutrition your body lost during childbirth and since. The ideal would be never to let the nutrients in your body get depleted to begin with—this is where taking prenatal vitamins comes in handy. The fact that you started supplementing specific vitamins and minerals you know you'll need extra of throughout your pregnancy means you'll be less nutrient-deficient than mothers who decided against supplementation.

Also, they may be called prenatal vitamins, but that doesn't mean you should stop taking them after bringing your baby into the world. It is recommended that you continue to take top-quality prenatal vitamins for two months or longer after childbirth. Remember, you'll be breastfeeding, so what I said earlier still applies: what you eat, your baby eats.

If you have a terrible case of the baby blues or even if you're suffering from full-blown postnatal depression, getting the correct balance of nutrients will help boost your mood. A happy mommy equals a happy baby.

The bottom line is, it doesn't mean now that you're no longer pregnant you should forget about your own health and focus only on your baby's.

## BREASTFEEDING

This is a personal decision to make. I know I was inundated with information and unsolicited advice when I had my first child. The thread that ran through all of this "advice" was that if you don't breastfeed your baby, then you're a bad mother. That's a very ignorant statement to make, considering that some babies can't tolerate breast milk. So, does that make them bad babies?

I'm not going to shame any woman who decides it is best for her baby to drink formula, but I am going to focus on the benefits of breastfeeding for you and your baby. What you end up choosing has nothing to do with anyone else.

**Breast milk contains an ideal mix of vitamins and minerals for your baby**. It is recommended that you breastfeed your baby for at least the first six months. But some mothers have gone on for much longer, precisely due to the nutritional content of breast milk.

**It is filled with essential antibodies.** This is particularly true of "first milk" produced the first few days after giving birth. It contains colostrum, which doesn't only provide immunoglobulin A (IgA), but it's also high in several other antibodies that will protect your little one from viruses and bacteria.

**Breastfeeding reduces your baby's risk of getting certain diseases.** When your  baby exclusively drinks breast milk, it is particularly beneficial to their health and cuts down their risk of getting:

- Middle ear infections
- Colds
- Respiratory tract infections
- Gut infections
- Intestinal tissue damage
- Allergies
- Sudden infant death syndrome

- Bowel diseases
- Childhood leukemia
- Diabetes

**It promotes a healthy weight.** Studies have shown that babies who were breastfed for longer than four months had a reduced chance of being over-weight or obese later in life (Grube et al., 2015). This is primarily due to the development of healthy gut bacteria, as well as having extra leptin in their bodies.

**Breast milk may boost your baby's intelligence.** Scientists believe the physical touch, eye contact, and intimacy that form part of breastfeeding have a significant impact on the brain development of infants (Brown, 2017).

**It helps your uterus contract after childbirth.** After giving birth, your body produces oxytocin—a bonding hormone. Oxytocin also helps to get your uterus back to the size it was before getting pregnant.

**It reduces your risk of getting specific diseases.** Just as with your baby, breastfeeding is linked with a reduced risk for:

- Breast and ovarian cancer
- Hypertension
- Arthritis
- Cholesterol
- Heart disease
- Type 2 Diabetes

**Breastfeeding saves time and money.**
Formula is expensive—breastfeeding in its most basic form is free. You also spend a lot of your time mixing and warming up formula milk and then have to clean and sterilize bottles.

## SUPPLEMENTS

I touched on the importance of continued supplementation after giving birth. Let's look at the five most critical nutrients you'll need to replenish after bringing a little human into this world and especially while you're breastfeeding.

Iron: You lose a lot of iron during childbirth. For your baby's optimal development, they'll need to get enough iron during breastfeeding, especially for their thyroid function. Eat red meat, liver, oysters, spinach, and kale, and you should have enough iron in your body for you and your baby.

Vitamin B12: If your baby is more irritable than usual, it may be a sign that you're not eating enough B12-rich foods. A deficiency of this specific hormone can impede your little one's development and lead to poor brain growth. Be sure to eat beef, liver, tuna, salmon, and clams. You can also up your B12 by consuming fortified dairy and cereals.

Omega-3 fatty acid: If you have a high concentrate of DHA in your breast milk, your baby's brain and eyes will be extra healthy. DHA is an excellent fat to supplement with no matter what the case since it enhances mental focus and decreases inflammation in the body. Salmon, sardines, fortified dairy, and eggs should be on your shopping list if you want to boost the DHA in your breast milk.

Choline: This nutrient is crucial for brain development, as well as infant memory. Eggs and organ meats will up your choline, but if you can't stomach that, get choline in pill form.

Vitamin D: What's better than spending some time outside with your baby, soaking up the sun? Just remember the sunscreen! If you're not the outdoorsy-type, fatty fish like salmon and tuna, fortified dairy, orange juice, liver, and egg yolks are excellent sources of vitamin D. Why do you need this vitamin? Well, it supports mommy and baby's immune system, brain and nervous system, and has the added benefit of preventing postnatal depression.

## LAB TESTING

You'll want to monitor your bundle of joy's health and development, and that is normal—but what about your health? After taking their first breath, babies are tested for almost everything under the sun. When it comes to postpartum testing, there is a lot of room for improvement. While we wait for the testing of new moms to gain traction, here are some labs that are essential to ensure you're recovering from giving birth and well enough to look after yourself and that new tiny family member of yours.

**Thyroid panel:** A properly functioning thyroid is vital to stabilizing your mood and preventing anxiety disorders. It helps maintain your energy levels and regulates your metabolic rates. Ask your doctor to perform a complete thyroid panel.

**Prolactin:** This hormone is known for its role in the production of breastmilk. To make sure you are producing enough milk for as long as possible, keep an eye on your prolactin levels.

**Vitamin D:** Since this nutrient plays such a vital role in boosting your immune system and reducing inflammation, you should ask your doctor to test for deficiencies. The test will most likely show that you require a supplement since a lot of people—not just women or pregnant women—don't have enough vitamin D in their bodies.

Getting these tests will help you assess your own health, which is a crucial step in measuring your baby's health. However, not all doctors will check these markers during your first postpartum visit. This doesn't mean you can't be your own health advocate and ask your doctor to organize these tests for you.

PHYSICAL RECOVERY

A big part of your physical recovery is getting fit and strong. Exercise is fundamental if you want to lose your baby weight healthily, but even more importantly, it's a natural antidepressant.

Some of the benefits of exercise after pregnancy includes:

- Weight loss
- Cardiovascular health
- Increased muscle mass
- Toning
- Boost energy levels
- Relieve stress
- Help you sleep
- Combat the baby blues
- Improves your mood

While you're breastfeeding, exercise will affect the volume you produce, as well as the composition of your milk. High-intensity exercise (not recommended soon after giving birth) may lead to an increase of lactic acid in the breast milk, which will give it a sour taste—one your baby might not like. I suggest you wait a few days after childbirth, if it was an uncomplicated vaginal delivery, and start incorporating some mild exercise in your day. If you had a C-section or some other complications during birth, your doctor will be the best person to tell you how long you should wait before getting active.

## LOVING YOUR BODY

There will be a lot of pressure on you to get your body
back to the way it was
before conceiving. Most of
the time, you'll be the one
applying the pressure, but I
want you to stop—you are
beautiful. It's vital for your
mental health to end any

self-loathing thoughts as soon as they creep up on
you. Now is the time for mom and baby to spend
time together and form an even deeper bond—there's
no room for breaking yourself down.

Pregnancy is life-changing—your body isn't immune
to this fact. But it has made your body stronger than
ever, so don't focus too much on your external
appearance. I want you to appreciate that over nine
months, you made magic. This should be your focus,
not your stretch marks or cellulite or baby fat.

Don't get me wrong. I'm not saying sit back and just
accept everything. There is nothing wrong with
wanting to lose some weight, but check your motives.

If it is about health and not because you think you're unattractive, then you're on the right track.

Here are some tips to help you lose those extra pounds.

1. Be realistic
2. Don't fall for crash or fad diets
3. Don't forget to exercise
4. Eat fewer calories than your body burns
5. Choose foods high in fiber

EMOTIONAL HEALTH

Having a baby is one of the most joyous experiences, but if we've learned anything in this book, it's that it can also be very stressful. Baby blues are a reality for a lot of women, and so is postnatal depression. There is a lot of focus on mindfulness during pregnancy throughout this book, but it doesn't stop there—you have to take care of your emotional and mental health now more than ever. If you don't, it will snowball, and before you know it, you'll find yourself in a deep, dark hole.

But, let's have a snowball fight!

*S* - *Sleep*
*N* - *Nutrition*
*O* – *Omega-3 fatty acids*
*W* - *Walking*
*B* – *Baby breaks*
*A* – *Adult time*
*L* - *Liquids*
*L* – *Laughter*

It looks easy on paper, but it will take a lot of commitment and effort from you, especially on the days when you don't even want to get out of bed.

## FAMILY PLANNING

If it is your and your partner's plan to have more than one child, you will have to sit down and plan. Yes, accidents do happen, but it is best to space pregnancies out.

Why is pregnancy spacing vital? Well, if you get pregnant within six months of giving birth, there is a risk of:

- Premature birth
- Placental abruption

- Low birth weight
- Schizophrenia
- Congenital disorders
- Maternal anemia
- Autism
- Inflammation of genital tract

It is best to wait 18 to 24 months between pregnancies. However, if you started late and you desperately want another baby before your clock runs out, you might consider waiting only 12 months. If that is the case, you will have to discuss any mitigating factors with your doctor and carefully follow their guidance. Your doctor is also the one who can recommend reliable birth control options to use in between pregnancies.

# 8

## BONUS: COMPLIMENTS TO
## THE CHEF

*J*t wouldn't be very thoughtful of me to end this book without including at least a few nutritious recipes for you to try! I think it is essential that you see that "healthy" doesn't equal "bland and boring." You will still be able to make fun and tasty meals and experiment in the kitchen. All you have to do is remember the fundamental concepts of a healthy diet: lots of fruits and veggies, eating enough fat and protein, avoiding refined carbs and sugary processed foods—basically keeping everything you put in your body as natural as possible.

The recipes below are tried-and-tested family favorites. I hope you enjoy them just as much as my family does.

Okay, momma, let's get cooking!

SOUPS & STEWS

Is there anything more satisfying than a thick and richly-flavored bowl of goodness? What I like most about soups and stews is the ability to cook a large quantity and freeze for a quick meal later.

## Garlic Sweet Potato and Lentil Soup

### *Ingredients (Makes 9 cups)*

- 1 tbsp olive oil
- ½ of a medium onion, diced
- 1 large celery stalk, sliced
- 1 medium red bell pepper, chopped

- 1 cup carrots, diced
- 2 garlic cloves, minced
- 1 tsp ground cumin
- ½ tsp ground coriander
- 2 tsp fresh thyme
- 2 cups lentils, rinsed
- 2 cans (approx. 4 cups) reduced-sodium chicken broth
- 1 can diced tomatoes
- 1 large sweet potato, peeled and cut into cubes

## Instructions

1. Add olive oil to a heavy pot and warm over medium heat. Mix in the chopped onion, celery, carrots, and red bell pepper. Stir for 3 minutes, then add the spices—garlic, thyme, cumin, and coriander. Cook until the vegetables are soft.
2. Next, add the broth, lentils, tomatoes, and sweet potato. Bring to a boil and then reduce heat and let simmer for 30 to 40 minutes. You can add more water to achieve the desired consistency. Stir often.

3. Pour ½ of the soup into a food processor or use an immersion blender to puree until smooth. Add the puree back to the original pot over low heat and stir until mixed. Serve.

## *Nutritional Values\* – 1 cup serving*

CALORIES - 230

PROTEIN - ½ SERVING

VITAMIN C1 - ½ SERVING

GREEN AND YELLOW VEGETABLES - 1 SERVING

WHOLE GRAINS - 2 SERVINGS

FAT, FIBER, IRON - SOME

*\*Values are based on recommended nutrient intake per meal. For example, ½ a cup of soup will meet your protein requirements for lunch/dinner.*

## Mother-In-Law's Hearty Beef Stew

### *Ingredients (Makes 8 to 9 cups)*

- 2 lb beef stewing meat cut into cubes
- 2 tbsp whole wheat flour
- 3 tbsp olive oil, divided
- 2 cans (approx. 4 cups) reduced-sodium beef broth
- 1 medium onion, diced
- 1 can chopped tomatoes
- 2 tsp dried thyme or 1 tbsp fresh thyme
- Salt and pepper to taste
- 6 carrots, peeled and cut into medium-sized chunks
- 3 medium boiling potatoes, peeled and cut into cubes
- ¼ cup minced parsley

## Instructions

Toss beef cubes in flour, salt, and pepper in a large bowl.

1. Add 1 tbsp oil to a heavy saucepan and heat. Add enough meat to cover the bottom of the pan and brown on all sides. Transfer beef back to the bowl. In the pot, add ¼ cup of broth and stir to scrape loose any meat

bits stuck to the bottom. Repeat this process until all the meat is browned.

2. Add the remaining oil to the pot. Add onions and stir for 5 minutes over medium-low heat. Add the beef cubes and juices back into the pan. Mix in the tomatoes, thyme, and remaining broth. You may have to add water to cover the meat. Increase the heat until contents reach boiling point. Then reduce heat to medium-low and allow to simmer for 1 hour.

3. Time to add the carrots and potatoes. Let it simmer with a closed lid for 45 minutes or until the beef is nice and tender, and the vegetables are fully cooked. Add water if you're not happy with the consistency. Garnish with parsley, and serve.

## Nutritional Values: 1-cup serving

CALORIES - 490

PROTEIN - 1 SERVING

VITAMIN C - ½ SERVING

GREEN AND YELLOW VEGETABLES - 2 SERVING

OTHER VEGETABLES - 1 SERVING

FAT - ½ SERVING

IRON - SOME

## Tomato and Basil Soup with Avocado

### *Ingredients (Serves 4)*

- 2 tsp olive oil
- 3 scallions, thinly diced
- Salt and pepper
- ½ tsp chopped garlic
- 4 medium-sized ripe tomatoes, seeded and chopped, or 1 ½ cups canned diced tomatoes with juice
- ¼ cup fresh basil, thinly sliced, or 2 tsp dried basil
- ½ red bell pepper, chopped
- Diced avocado and 4 lime wedges for serving

## Instructions

1. Heat the olive oil over medium heat. Add the garlic and scallions to the pan and cook until soft.
2. Add the basil, red bell pepper, tomatoes, and tomato juice and raise the heat to medium-high. Once the ingredients come to a boil, reduce the heat and let simmer for 15 minutes. Add salt and pepper to taste.
3. Pour the soup into serving bowls and add the avocado on top. Add the lime wedges to the side.

### *Nutritional Values: 1 bowl*

CALORIES - 119

VITAMIN C - 2 ½ SERVING

GREEN AND YELLOW VEGETABLES AND FRUITS - 1 ½ SERVING

SALAD

I used to think salad meant lettuce and a few other added ingredients to add at least some taste. Boy, was I wrong! You can get creative with what you eat, and better yet, lettuce does not have to be the base. Instead of lettuce, use spinach or kale, or how about a pumpkin and basil salad? Only your imagination is your salad's limit!

## Arugula, Cucumber, and Mint Salad

### *Ingredients (Serves 2)*

- 1 bunch arugula, washed
- ½ large cucumber, peeled, seeded, and diced
- 2 tbsp fresh mint, chopped
- ½ mango, peeled and diced
- 2 to 3 tbsp salad dressing of choice

## Instructions

1. Toss arugula, cucumber, and mint in a large serving bowl.
2. Add salad dressing and mix. Serve with mango on top.

## Nutritional Values: 1 serving

CALORIES - 125

VITAMIN C - ½ SERVING

GREEN AND YELLOW VEGETABLES - 2 SERVING

OTHER VEGETABLES - 1/2 SERVING

FAT - ½ SERVING

## Spinach and Soybean Pod Salad with Parmesan Shavings

## *Ingredients (Serves 2)*

- 1 cup frozen edamame
- 4 cups baby spinach leaves, rinsed
- 2 tbsp citrus-based salad dressing
- ½ cup Parmesan cheese, coarsely grated

## *Instructions*

1. Bring water to boil over high heat. Add the edamame and leave to cook for 4 minutes. Drain and rinse with cold water to stop the cooking process. Pat dry.
2. Mix the spinach, edamame, and salad dressing in a medium bowl. Serve with a sprinkling of Parmesan on top.

## *Nutritional Values: 1 serving*

CALORIES - 240

PROTEIN - ½ SERVING

VITAMIN C - ½ SERVING

CALCIUM - 1 SERVING

GREEN AND YELLOW VEGETABLES - 1 SERVING

FAT - ½ SERVING

## Caesar Salad With an Ocean Twist

### *Ingredients (Serves 2)*

- 12 jumbo shrimp, shelled and deveined
- 4 cups shredded romaine lettuce
- 1 medium-size bell pepper, thinly sliced
- 1 cup small cherry tomatoes
- ½ cup grated Parmesan
- 2 tbsp Caesar dressing (see below)
- Olive oil cooking spray
- Black pepper to taste
- Lemon wedges for serving

### *Instructions*

1. Coat a skillet with cooking spray and bring to high heat. In a bowl, season the shrimp with black pepper. Once the pan is hot, add the shrimp and cook for 4 minutes or however long it takes to cook through. Set shrimp aside.

2. Add the lettuce, bell pepper, tomatoes, and Parmesan cheese to a bowl, and mix in the salad dressing.

3. Divide salad between 2 plates and top with 8 shrimp each. Add more Parmesan if desired and serve with lemon wedges.

## *Nutritional Values: 1 serving without dressing*

CALORIES - 470

PROTEIN - 1 SERVING

VITAMIN C - 4 SERVINGS

CALCIUM - 1 SERVING

GREEN AND YELLOW VEGETABLES AND FRUITS - 3 SERVINGS

### *Caesar Dressing*

Traditionally, Caesar dressing contains raw egg. Since that is not good for pregnant or breastfeeding women, here is an eggless version

### *Ingredients (Makes ½ cup)*

- 1 tsp chopped garlic
- 4 tbsp fresh lemon juice
- 2 tbsp olive oil (add more to taste)
- ½ cup grated Parmesan cheese (add more to taste)
- Salt and black pepper to taste
- Optional: 2 anchovy fillets, drained and coarsely chopped

## Instructions

Add all the ingredients to a blender or food processor and puree—season with salt and black pepper.

## Nutritional Values: ¼ cup serving

CALORIES - 196

VITAMIN C - 1/2 SERVING

CALCIUM - 1/2 SERVING

FATS - 1 ½ SERVING

POULTRY

Protein is a vital macronutrient, but after fish, poultry is the next healthiest protein source. You can swap red meat for chicken or turkey in almost all recipes. Also, gone are the days of bland chicken breasts—you'll soon find out just how flavorsome your poultry dishes can be.

## Turkey Cutlets Soaked in Mushroom Sauce

### Ingredients (Serves 2)

- Whole wheat flour
- 2, 6 ounce and ½-inch thick turkey cutlets
- Salt and pepper to taste
- Olive oil cooking spray
- 1 tsp olive oil
- 2 tsp butter
- 2 shallots, minced
- ½ pound (3 cups) sliced mushrooms
- 1 cup shredded carrots
- ½ cup frozen peas
- 1 tsp fresh tarragon, minced
- 2 tbsp parsley, chopped
- 3 tbsp fresh chives, snipped
- ¾ cup low-sodium chicken or vegetable broth

## Instructions

1. Season the turkey with salt and pepper and then cover each cutlet with flour on both sides.
2. Spray a large skillet with the cooking spray and add 1 teaspoon of the olive oil into the skillet. Heat over medium heat. Add the cutlets and cook until browned but not

completely done, 2 minutes per side should do. Remove cutlets from the skillet.

3. Coat the pan again with cooking spray and melt the butter over medium-low heat. Cook the shallots for 2 minutes until slightly soft. Turn up the heat to medium-high and add the mushrooms; cook for a further 2 minutes.

4. Add the peas, carrots, chives, parsley, tarragon, and broth and bring to a boil. Lower the heat and let simmer for 3 minutes. At this point, return the turkey cutlets to the skillet. Let simmer while frequently stirring until the sauce is reduced and the turkey is thoroughly cooked. Season with salt and pepper and garnish with parsley and chives.

## *Nutritional Values: 1 portion*

CALORIES - 245

PROTEIN - 1 ½ SERVING

GREEN LEAFY AND YELLOW VEGETABLES AND FRUITS - 2 SERVINGS

OTHER VEGETABLES AND FRUITS - 3 SERVINGS

## Thai Sesame Chicken Bowl

This is delicious served on a bed of quinoa.

### *Ingredients (Serves 1)*

*Sesame sauce*

- 1 tsp rice vinegar
- 1 tsp sesame oil
- 1 tsp reduced-sodium soy sauce
- ½ tsp Asian sesame oil
- 1 tbsp sesame seeds

*Vegetables*

- 1 cup baby carrots
- 1 stalk broccoli
- ½ cup green beans or snow peas

*Chicken*

- 4 oz pre-cooked chicken

## *Instructions*

1. Combine vinegar, soy sauces, and sesame oils in a medium bowl and whisk until combined. Set aside.

2. Trim the broccoli stalks into florets and cut in half vertically. Halve the beans (if you're using any). Start to steam the broccoli and beans over boiling water, covering for 8 minutes. After 3 minutes have passed, add the carrots to the broccoli. Wait a further 4 minutes and then add the snow peas.

3. In a large bowl, toss all the vegetables with the oil. Cut the pre-cooked chicken into cubes and mix in. Serve hot over quinoa or brown rice and garnish with sesame seeds.

## *Nutritional Values: 1 serving*

CALORIES - 685

PROTEIN - 2 SERVINGS

VITAMIN C - 2 SERVINGS

GREEN AND YELLOW VEGETABLES AND FRUITS - 3 SERVINGS

WHOLE GRAINS - 1 SERVING

FAT - 1 SERVING

## Homemade Chicken Pita

### *Ingredients (Serves 1)*

- ¾ cup diced chicken or turkey (pre-cooked)
- 3 tbsp plain yogurt
- 2 tsp mayonnaise
- ¼ cup ¼-inch thick slices seedless cucumber
- 1 plum tomato, diced
- 1 tsp fresh cilantro, chopped
- ½ tsp curry powder
- Pinch of ground cumin
- Salt and pepper to taste
- Hot sauce (optional)
- 1 whole-wheat pita
- ½ cup arugula rinsed and patted dry or ½ cup coleslaw mix
- 1 tbsp raisins
- 1 tbsp roasted sunflower seeds

## *Instructions*

1. Put chicken, mayonnaise, yogurt, cucumber, tomato, curry powder, cilantro, and cumin into a bowl and mix. Season with salt and pepper to taste and add hot sauce.
2. Fill the pita with arugula and add the chicken mix. Garnish with raisins and sunflower seeds.

## *Nutritional Values: 1 portion*

CALORIES - 336

PROTEIN - 1 SERVING

VITAMIN C - ½ SERVING

GREEN AND YELLOW VEGETABLES AND FRUITS - ½ SERVING

WHOLE GRAINS AND LEGUMES - 2 SERVINGS

FAT - ½ SERVING

## BEEF AND SEAFOOD

You can't live on chicken and turkey, am I right? That would get very boring for your taste buds after a while. Red meat isn't all bad; it depends on the cut of meat and how you cook it. And when it comes to seafood, you can't go wrong–well, unless you eat fish that's high in mercury, of course.

### Tortilla Lasagna

### *Ingredients (Serves 6)*

- 2 tsp olive oil
- 1 medium onion, chopped
- 1 medium red bell pepper, diced
- 2 cloves garlic, minced

- 1 pound extra-lean ground beef
- ¾ cup carrots, grated
- 1 tbsp chili powder
- 1 ½ tsp ground cumin
- 1 tbsp fresh oregano, chopped, or 1 teaspoon dried oregano
- 1 cup frozen yellow corn kernels
- 1 cup enchilada sauce
- 1 can Mexican-style tomato sauce
- 1 container low-fat cottage cheese
- 2 large eggs, lightly beaten
- ¼ cup Parmesan cheese, grated
- Black pepper to taste
- Olive oil cooking spray
- 12 corn or whole wheat flour tortillas
- 1 ½ cups cheddar cheese, finely shredded
- Optional: Sour cream or plain yogurt, fresh cilantro, chopped tomato, and black olives for serving

## Instructions

1. Preheat the oven to 375 degrees Fahrenheit.
2. Warm the oil in a nonstick skillet over

medium heat. Add the onion, garlic, and bell pepper and cook for 5 minutes. Mix in the carrots, beef, chili powder, cumin, and oregano and cook until everything is cooked through (about 10 minutes). Add the corn, enchilada sauce, and tomato sauce and let simmer for 5 minutes. Stir frequently during this time.

3. Place the eggs, Parmesan cheese, and cottage cheese in a bowl and mix. Season with black pepper and set aside.

4. Coat a baking dish (13-by-9-inch) with olive oil spray and pack 6 of the tortillas at the bottom. Spread the beef mixture over the tortillas, followed by the cottage cheese paste. Add the remaining 6 tortillas on top and cover with the remaining meat mixture.

5. Bake for 20 minutes. Sprinkle cheddar cheese over the top and put the dish back in the oven for a further 10 minutes until the cheese is melted.

6. Let the lasagna stand for 10 minutes, then top with yogurt, cilantro, tomato, or olives if desired.

### *Nutritional Values: 1 portion*

CALORIES - 384

PROTEIN - 1 ½ SERVING

CALCIUM - 1 SERVING

VITAMIN C - 1 SERVING

GREEN AND YELLOW VEGETABLES AND FRUITS - 1 SERVING

OTHER VEGETABLES AND FRUITS - 1 SERVING

WHOLE GRAINS AND LEGUMES - 2 SERVINGS

## **Basil and Tomato Flavored Salmon**

### *Ingredients (Serves 2)*

- Olive oil cooking spray
- 12 cherry tomatoes, halved
- 12 fresh basil leaves
- 1 tbsp olive oil
- 2 skinless salmon fillets (6 ounces)
- Salt and black pepper to taste

## *Instructions*

1. Preheat the oven to 450 degrees Fahrenheit.
2. Tear off two 12-inch-long pieces of heavy-duty aluminum foil and coat with cooking spray.
3. Place one piece of salmon in the center of each strip of foil. Top each with half of the cherry tomatoes and 6 basil leaves. Trickle 1 teaspoon of olive oil over each piece of salmon and season with salt and pepper.
4. Fold the foil to close but leave room for heat to circulate inside before crimping the edges shut tight. Don't leave any gaps where juices can leak out.
5. Place foil packets on a baking sheet and bake for 15-20 minutes depending on the thickness of the salmon fillets. If you're not sure when the salmon is done, carefully open one foil packet and pierce the salmon with a fork. If cooked, it will flake easily and be a light pink color inside. Serve with a side of your choice.

### *Nutritional Values: 1 portion*

CALORIES - 240

PROTEIN - 1 ½ SERVING

VITAMIN C - 1 SERVING

FAT - ½ SERVING

## Beefy Meal On a Stick

### *Ingredients (Serves 4)*

- ½ pound lean beef cut into 1-inch pieces
- 12 cherry or grape tomatoes
- 1 medium red onion cut into 2-inch pieces
- 12 white button mushrooms, caps only, washed
- 2 tbsp low-sodium soy sauce
- 2 tbsp fresh lemon juice
- 1 tbsp olive oil
- 1 tsp ground cumin

### *Instructions*

1. Put the beef, olive oil, lemon juice, soy

sauce, and cumin in a bowl and toss until beef cubes are coated evenly. Cover the bowl and refrigerate for 3 hours or overnight.
2. Prepare the grill or preheat the broiler.
3. Thread the marinated beef onto 8 skewers, alternating with the mushrooms, tomatoes, bell pepper, and onion.
4. Grill or broil until beef is cooked but still tender.

If you want a sweeter tasting marinade, use 2 table-spoons of pineapple juice concentrate instead or the lemon juice. You can also use pineapple and mango chunks in place of the mushrooms and tomatoes.

## *Nutritional Values: 1 portion*

CALORIES - 252

PROTEIN - 1 SERVING

VITAMIN C - 2 ½ SERVINGS

GREEN AND YELLOW VEGETABLES AND FRUITS - 1 SERVING

OTHER VEGETABLES AND FRUITS - I ½ SERVING

IRON - BEEF

## VEGETARIAN AND VEGAN

I didn't forget about our plant-based mommies. Two days a week, we eat vegetarian at my house. It's healthy, and we save some money while saving the earth! It doesn't matter if you're vegetarian for ethical reasons, or if you have a condition that is better managed with a plant-based diet, you can still eat like the queens you are.

·  ·  ·

## Veg and Cheese

### Ingredients (Serves 4)

- ½ lb whole wheat or soy pasta, small shapes
- 2 tbsp butter
- 1 cup milk
- 1 ½ tbsp whole-wheat flour
- 1 cup cheddar cheese, shredded
- 1 cup mozzarella cheese, shredded
- 2 tbsp Parmesan cheese, grated
- 1 tbsp wheat germ
- 1 cup frozen peas, thawed
- ½ cup cooked carrot pieces

### Instructions

1. Preheat the oven to 350 degrees Fahrenheit.
2. Cook the pasta according to package instructions.
3. In a small nonstick saucepan, melt the butter over medium heat. Add the flour to form a paste and slowly add the milk, all the while stirring briskly. Let the mixture simmer until it thickens slightly. Pour the

white sauce of the cheddar and mozzarella cheese in a separate bowl and stir to combine.

4. Place peas in a colander and drain the pasta over the peas. The head of the water will be enough to cook the peas. Gently mix the pasta, peas, and cooked carrots into the cheese sauce and pour the mixture into a round casserole

5. Combine the Parmesan and wheat germ and sprinkle over the pasta. Bake for 10 minutes.

## Nutritional Values: 1 serving

CALORIES - 340

PROTEIN - 1 ½ SERVING

CALCIUM - 2 ½ SERVINGS

GREEN AND YELLOW VEGETABLES AND FRUITS - ½ SERVING

OTHER VEGETABLES AND FRUITS - ½ SERVING

WHOLE GRAINS - 2 SERVINGS

FAT - ½ SERVING

## Asian Tofu, Peas and Peppers Bowl

### Ingredients (Serves 2)

- 2 tbsp oyster sauce
- 1 tbsp reduced-sodium chicken broth
- 1 tsp rice vinegar
- 1 tsp Asian sesame oil
- 1 tsp cornstarch
- 3 tsp olive oil, divided
- 10 oz extra-firm tofu cut into 1-inch cubes
- 1 stalk broccoli
- ½ medium bell pepper, thinly diced
- 1 cup snow peas
- 2 tbsp fresh ginger, minced
- 2 tbsp scallions, thinly diced

### Instructions

1. Mix oyster sauce, vinegar, sesame oil, broth, and cornstarch.
2. Heat 2 teaspoons of the olive oil in a wok or nonstick skillet over medium heat. Add tofu and cook until light golden (3 minutes per side). Add 1/3 cup water and the broccoli into the wok and bring it to simmer until

the broccoli is cooked. Remove the tofu and broccoli from the pan and put aside.

3. Add the remaining olive oil to the wok and warm over medium heat. Add the bell pepper and cook for 3 minutes. Next, insert the snow peas, ginger, and the oyster sauce mixture. Cook for 1 minute while continuously stirring. Eat as is or serve over rice. Garnish with scallions.

## *Nutritional Values: 1 serving*

Calories - 220

Protein - ½ serving

Calcium - 1 serving

Green and yellow vegetables - 1 serving

Other vegetables - 1 serving

Fat - ½ serving

## Omelet Filled With Cheesy Broccoli

### *Ingredients (Serves 1)*

- 2 large eggs

- Salt and black pepper to taste
- 2 tsp cold water
- 1 tsp olive oil
- ¼ cheddar cheese, shredded
- ½ cup broccoli florets, cooked

## Instructions

1. Whisk eggs together, add water, salt, and pepper, and whisk for another 10 seconds.
2. In a nonstick skillet, add the oil and warm over medium-high heat. Reduce the heat and add the egg mixture. Cook until the eggs are set. Use a spatula to lift the edge around the perimeter of the pan to let the uncooked egg run underneath.
3. Cook for a further 2 minutes, then add the cheese on top. Cook for about 1 minute then spoon the broccoli onto one half of the omelet. Fold the other half of the egg over and slide onto a plate. Eat while hot.

## Nutritional Values: 1 serving

CALORIES - 450

PROTEIN - 1 SERVING

CALCIUM - 1 SERVING

VITAMIN C - 1 SERVING

GREEN AND YELLOW VEGETABLES - 1 SERVING

FAT - ½ SERVING

# LEAVE A 1-CLICK REVIEW!

*I would be incredibly thankful if you could take just 60 seconds to write a brief review on Amazon, even if it's just a couple sentences!*

**SCAN QR CODE ABOVE OR VISIT LINK BELOW:**
http://www.amazon.com/review/create-review?&
asin=B08LCRJW2Q

CONCLUSION

Pregnancy—what a roller coaster ride. It starts when you first see the positive test result. Your mind races a mile a minute: "Will I make a good mom?" "How will I care for a baby?" "What about my finances?" The questions start then and will be with you throughout your pregnancy. On top of that, you'll dream up worst-case scenarios about your baby's health and childbirth that will drive you mad.

I have to say, for all the good that comes with pregnancy, there sure is a lot of bad. Heartburn, swollen feet, backache, sciatica, fatigue, moodiness, nausea, the list goes on. How do we do it?

Well, I'll tell you how. By being the strong women we have come to be. The only thing we really need help with is wading through heaps and heaps of information, deciding what is factual and up-to-date, and applying it to our pregnancy. It's a challenging task if you don't know where to begin. But, you picked *Table for Two*, and I can't tell you how ecstatic I am to have gone on this journey with you.

I agonized over every single tiny detail of my first pregnancy and devoured pregnancy book after pregnancy book while snacking on that particular day's bizarre craving. It was tiring. That is why I set out to write this book—to save you the anxiety of figuring out what information is the best for you and your little one.

That's one thing you may have noticed: pregnancy is all about managing your stress levels and staying calm and relaxed. By finding ways to stay in the here and now, you will be able to put any anxious feelings at bay. This makes complete sense if you consider the places your mind will wander if left unattended.

If this is your first pregnancy, mindfulness is especially essential to cope with all your fears. If you don't, it will lead to self-doubt, and from there will spiral into repeated negativity that will suck all the joy out of being pregnant.

I think if someone were to ask me what the key to a happy pregnancy is, I'd say taking care of the mom-to-be. If you think about it, everything you do impacts that little life growing inside of you. If you're stressed, it sets off reactions in your body which, in turn, influence your baby's development. A lot of first-time moms don't see things this way around—they are so focused on taking care of the life growing inside them that they forget about themselves. This is a total counterintuitive approach to a healthy pregnancy.

If mommy feels good, the tiny little human in her tummy will, too! So, neglecting your own needs is actually harmful to your baby, you see?

One of the easiest ways to take care of yourself is through nutrition. If you eat a balanced diet, a lot of things in your body will fall into place. Remember that your baby is a nutrient thief, and you'll have to make up for everything they're stealing by eating a lot of fruits and vegetables, protein, fat, and complex carbs. In most cases, you may need to add some supplements on top of an already healthy diet. I can't say enough good things about prenatal vitamins. They're like magic pills packed with all the goodies you and the life inside you need; folic acid, iron, calcium, vitamin D, and vitamins C, A, B, and E, as well as zinc and iodine. But don't forget to throw some omega-3 fatty acids into the mix too.

When all is said and done, I want you to take care of yourself without feeling an ounce of guilt for doing so! Eating the right foods, staying active, and limiting stress will all count toward giving birth to a healthy baby. I will repeat what I said in the introduction of this book: what is good for you, will be good for the baby.

But, before you leave to go relax in a warm bath because your baby said so, I want to emphasize some ways you can savor this wonderful time in your life.

*1. Say yes*

Everyone loves helping a pregnant lady. So, stick your pride in your mommy jeans pocket and accept their help. If someone wants to carry your grocery bags, let them. You can pay back this gesture of kindness by helping a pregnant woman in the future.

*2. Avoid nesting stress*

I enjoyed so much going shopping for a new crib, toys, and accessories for the nursery. But it became a little overwhelming after a while, and I had to take a step back and remind myself that my little one just needed a room over their head, essential clothing, food, diapers, and my love. Keep that in mind when you come face to face with two shades of yellow, and you can't decide between them.

*3. Don't neglect your looks*

If you look good, you feel good. Go shopping for some maternity outfits (don't forget pretty lingerie), and get dressed to impress. This will give you a much-needed confidence boost because we tend to feel like ugly ducklings once we can't see our feet. Thanks, baby bump!

*4. Get spiritual*

We covered this in the mindfulness chapter. Find something that brings you peace. It doesn't have to be anything religious (unless you want it to be), but if it is something that brings you more in tune with creation and nature, you'll be more accepting of what life has to offer.

*5. Get motivated by your health*

Yes, *your* health. Start forming healthy habits that will be with you long after childbirth. If you decide to exercise because you know it will be good for you, then you'll continue doing it whether there's a baby in your belly or not. Your baby will benefit from these new healthy habits, too.

*6. Have more sex*

I realize your libido will be all over the place, but pregnancy can be sexy. Your senses are heightened, different hormones mean different reactions and sensations, and, bonus, you don't have to worry about getting pregnant! It is the perfect time to try new positions, get creative with lingerie, or just connect with your partner on a deeper, more honest level. If you can discuss your sexual relationship during this time, maybe you can figure out areas where things were lacking before.

*7. Grow your circle of friends*

Between the doctor's waiting room, breathing classes, yoga, and all the other places soon-to-be mommies hang out, you have enough access to possible BFFs. What's more, you will have an immediate connection with women you meet here because you're sharing the same experience. Who better to ask for hints and tips than someone who has been through the same thing?

## 8. Be more romantic

If there ever was a time for you and your partner to take that romantic trip to the family cabin at the lake, it's now. It's still only the two of you, a luxury that you won't have for 18 or more years after your baby comes into the world. Spend time together, talk about your hopes and fears about being parents, what support you need, and how you each think the baby will change your relationship. This level of communication will foster understanding and will last long after you've given birth.

## 9. Explore exercise

Before you got pregnant, you most likely hit the cardio machines or did some weight lifting. However, when there's a tiny human inside you, you'll have to reassess how you approach exercise.

Now is the ideal time to explore new types of exercise. What about some prenatal yoga, pool aerobics, or exercises geared to assisting you in labor?

10. *Hide your scale*

Now is not the time to obsess about your weight. The water in your body will fluctuate so much, and you might pick up a pound in one day only to lose it the following. Also, you're pregnant, so you're supposed to gain weight—a healthy amount, that is. I suggest you limit weighing yourself to once every two weeks, or once a week tops!

11. *Focus on your baby*

I found that the fastest way to snap me out of feeling sorry for myself while I was pregnant was to think about the human growing inside me. When I got tired of the constant backache, I reminded myself that soon I'd be sitting comfortably in a rocking chair, while holding my sweet-smelling little angel in my arms. This put the pain I was experiencing into perspective. After all, you can't expect to build a whole new human without feeling some discomfort, right?

As you can see, being pregnant can be fun! It's all in your approach. If you enter this phase of your life with a positive attitude and an upbeat outlook, things will magically fall into place! It's easier said than done when you have pregnancy hormones working against you, but it's not impossible.

At the beginning of *Table for Two*, I set out to answer some of the burning questions soon-to-be mommies ask—from questioning their parenting skills, being afraid of what will happen to their bodies, what to eat, to how to cope with depression and more. I hope I did just that, and you found this book an informative guide to pregnancy—whether it's your first, second, or third.

If you did find this book helpful, please share it with friends and family members who you think may gain something from reading it. I want to take as much of the guesswork out of being pregnant as possible so that women can focus on the positive aspects.

Before I leave you, please give this book a favorable review so that more women can have access to what I hope is an ultimate modern-day guide to pregnancy.

## 14 Baby Essentials Every Mom Must Have...

*This checklist includes:*

- 14 ESSENTIALS THAT YOU DIDN'T KNOW YOU NEEDED FOR YOUR LITTLE ONE AND YOURSELF
- ITEMS WHICH WILL MAKE BEING A MAMA BEAR EASIER
- WHERE YOU CAN PURCHASE THESE ITEMS AT THE LOWEST PRICE

The last thing you want to do is be unprepared and unequipped to give your little one an enjoyable and secure environment to grow up in. It is never too late to prepare for this!

*To receive your free Mommy Checklist,*
*visit the link or scan the QR code below:*

https://purelypublishing.activehosted.com/f/1

Elizabeth Newborne is an established nutritionist and loving mother of three. She has devoted her life to helping mothers understand how to take care of themselves and their little ones, both inside the womb during pregnancy and outside, as they guide their newborns through the developmental stages of life. It is her passion to share with you everything she has learned from bringing into the world her two wonderful boys and her sweet little girl, to her two decades of knowledge in physical and psychological health and nutrition. She has coached and guided countless women through their pregnancies and helped mothers become the best version of themselves for their newborns and families, giving them access to the information she wishes she had when she was a new mother.

Her knowledge as a respected nutritionist, combined with her personal experience as a mother, makes her one of the leading experts on healthy and happy pregnancies and motherhood.

www.facebook.com/groups/modernsupermom
www.instagram.com/elizabethnewborne
elizabeth@newbornepublishing.com

# REFERENCES

Adams, S.S., Eberhard-Gran, M. & Eskild, A. (2012). Fear of childbirth and duration of labour: a study of 2206 women with intended vaginal delivery. *BJOG*, 119, 1238-1246. https://doi.org/10.1111/j.1471-0528.2012.03433.x

American pregnancy associations. (n.d.). *Pregnancy Weight Gain*. https://americanpregnancy.org/pregnancy-health/pregnancy-weight-gain-968

BMJ. (n.d.). Women taking probiotics during pregnancy might have lower preeclampsia and premature birth risk. https://www.bmj.com/company/newsroom/women-taking-probiotics-during-pregnancy-might-have-lower-pre-eclampsia-and-premature-birth-risk/

Brantsaeter, A. L., Torjusen, H., Meltzer, H. M., Papadopoulou, E., Hoppin, J. A., Alexander, J., Lieblein, G., Roos, G., Holten, J. M., Swartz, J. & Haugen, M. (2016). Organic food consumption during pregnancy and hypospadias and cryptorchidism at birth: The Norwegian Mother and Child Cohort Study (MoBa). *Environmental Health Perspectives*, 124(3), 357–364. https://doi.org/10.1289/ehp.1409518

Brown, B.M. (2017). The science of breastfeeding and brain development. *Breastfeeding Medicine*, 12(8), 459–461. https://doi.org/10.1089/bfm.2017.0122

Browne, P.D., Bolte, A., Claassen, E., De Weerth, E. (2019). Probiotics in pregnancy: Protocol of a double-blind randomized controlled pilot trial for pregnant women with depression and anxiety. *Trials*, 20, 440. https://doi.org/10.1186/s13063-019-3389-1

Cameron, E.L. (2014). Pregnancy and olfaction: A review. *Frontiers in Psychology*, 5: 67. https://doi.org/10.3389/fpsyg.2014.00067

Centers for Disease control and Prevention. (n.d.). Preterm Birth. https://www.cdc.gov/

reproductivehealth/
maternalinfanthealth/pretermbirth.htm

Cheng, E.R., Rifas-Shiman, S.L., Perkins, M.E.,
Rich-Edwards, J.W., Gillman, M.W., Wright, R. &
Taveras, E.M. (2016). The influence of antenatal
partner support on pregnancy outcomes. *Journal of
Women's Health*, 25(7):672-679. https://doi.org/10.
1089/jwh.2015.5462

Clapp, J.F. (2002). Maternal carbohydrate intake
and pregnancy outcome. The Proceedings of the
Nutritional Society, 61(1), 45-50. https://doi.org/10.
1079/pns2001129

Cleveland Clinic. (n.d.). Heart healthy eating to help
lower cholesterol levels. https://my.clevelandclinic.
org/health/articles/17281-heart-healthy-eating-to-
help-lower-cholesterol-levels

Duncan, L.G., Cohn, M.A., Chao, M.T., Cook, J.G.,
Riccobono, J. & Bardacke, N. (2017) Benefits of
preparing for childbirth with mindfulness training: a
randomized controlled trial with active comparison.
*BMC Pregnancy Childbirth*, 17, 140. https://doi.org/
10.1186/s12884-017-1319-3

Dunn, C., Hanieh, E., Roberts, R. & Powrie, R. (2012). Mindful pregnancy and childbirth: Effects of a mindfulness-based intervention on women's psychological distress and well-being in the perinatal period. *Archives of Women's Mental Health*, 15, 139–143. https://doi.org/10.1007/s00737-012-0264-4

Figure 10: Campo, I. (2017). Pregnant woman wearing a blue panty [Photograph]. *Unsplash.* https://unsplash.com/photos/FKOjXAbJWlw

Figure 11: Larke, B. (2017). Black and red cherries on white bowl [Photograph]. *Unsplash.* https://unsplash.com/photos/nTZOILVZuOg

Figure 12: Olsson, E. (2018). Veggies on blue surface [Photograph]. *Unsplash.* https://unsplash.com/photos/7EhPbdAQG-s

Figure 13: Braun, L. (2019). Woman carries baby [Photograph]. *Unsplash.* https://unsplash.com/photos/hdmGreHJPZ8

Figure 14: Kosar, J. (2020). Bowl of thick soup on plate [Photograph]. *Unsplash.* https://unsplash.com/photos/k5VGs9qQubc

Figure 15: Aziz, Y. (2019). Vegetable salad in gray bowl [Photograph]. *Unsplash.* https://unsplash.com/photos/AiHJiRCwB3w

Figure 16: Like Meat. (2020). Fried meat with green vegetables on black plate [Photograph]. *Unsplash.* https://unsplash.com/photos/f96pzsJZpcs

Figure 17: Minh, T.N.(2018). Shallow focus photo of grilled barbeque [Photograph]. *Unsplash.* https://unsplash.com/photos/vK6B4fBR464

Figure 18: Sonn, Jo. (2018). Cooked rice with vegetable salad in brown wooden bowl [Photograph]. *Unsplash.* https://unsplash.com/photos/M-tzZD5z720

Figure 1: Borba, J. (2020). Free Apparel Image [Photograph]. *Unsplash.* https://unsplash.com/photos/cwgCZu96q6s

Figure 2: McCutcheon, S. (2020). Pink heart lollipop on white textile [Photograph]. *Unsplash.* https://unsplash.com/photos/8XkNFQG_cgk

Figure 3: Hanaoka, P. (2017). Woman carrying baby [Photograph]. *Unsplash.* https://unsplash.com/photos/a1o4tlUezug

Figure 4: De Lotz, G. (2020). Happy birthday with white and yellow flowers [Photograph]. *Unsplash.* https://unsplash.com/photos/HoD2lHLYhaw

Figure 5: De Boekhorst, M. (2018). Shadow of woman on bed [Photograph]. *Unsplash.* https://unsplash.com/photos/3sn9MUlx2ZE

Figure 9: Conscious Design. (2020). Women in brown knit sweater holding brown ceramic cup [Photograph]. *Unsplash.* https://unsplash.com/photos/VsI_74zRzA

Gete, D.G., Waller, M. & Mishra, G.D. (2020. Prepregnancy dietary patterns and risk of preterm birth and low birth weight: Findings from the Australian Longitudinal Study on Women's Health. *The American Journal of Clinical Nutrition,* 111(5), 1048–1058. https://doi.org/10.1093/ajcn/nqaa057

Grube, M.M., Von der Lippe, E., Schlaud, M. & Brettschneider, A.K. (2015). Does breastfeeding help to reduce the risk of childhood overweight and obesity? A propensity score analysis of data from the KiGGS Study. *PLoS ONE,* 10(4). https://doi.org/10.1371/journal.pone.0126675

Hedderson, M.M., Ferrara, A., Avalos, L.A., Van den Eeden, S.K., Gunderson, E.P., Li, D.K., Altschuler, A., Woo, S., Rowell, S., Choudhary, V., Xu,F., Flanagan, T., Schaefer, C. & Croen, C. (2016). The Kaiser Permanente Northern California research program on genes, environment, and health (RPGEH) pregnancy cohort: Study design, methodology and baseline characteristics. *BMC Pregnancy Childbirth*, 16, 381. https://doi.org/10.1186/s12884-016-1150-2

Johnson, P., Mount, K. & Graziano, S. (2014). Functional bowel disorders in pregnancy: Effect on quality of life, evaluation and management. *AOGS*. https://doi.org/10.1111/aogs.12434

Kapadia, M.Z., Park, C.K,. Beyene, J., Giglia, L., Maxwell, C. & McDonald, S.D. (2015). Weight loss instead of weight gain within the guidelines in obese women during pregnancy: A systematic review and meta-analyses of maternal and infant outcomes. *Public Library of Science*, 10(7). https://doi.org/10.1371/journal.pone.0132650

Kashanian, M., Faghankhani, M., Roshan, M.Y., Pour, M.E. & Sheikhansari, N. (2019). Woman's perceived stress during pregnancy; stressors and pregnancy adverse outcomes. *The Journal of Maternal-Fetal & Neonatal Medicine.* https://doi.org/10.1080/14767058.2019.1602600

Kondo, S., Tayama, K., Tsukamoto, Y., Ikeda, K. & Yamoni, Y. (2001). Antihypertensive effects of acetic acid and vinegar on spontaneously hypertensive rats. *Bioscience, Biotechnology, and Biochemistry*, 65(12), 2690-2694. https://doi.org/10.1271/bbb.65.2690

Kumar, P. & Magon, N. (2012). Hormones in pregnancy. *Nigerian Medical Journal*, 53(4), 179–183. https://doi.org/10.4103/0300-1652.107549

Mennella, J. A., Jagnow, C. P. & Beauchamp, G. K. (2001). Prenatal and postnatal flavor learning by human infants. *Pediatrics*, 107(6). https://doi.org/10.1542/peds.107.6.e88

Mohammadbeigi, R., Shahgeibi, S., Soufizadeh, N., Rezaiie, M. & Farhadifar, F. (2011). Comparing the effects of ginger and metoclopramide on the treatment of pregnancy nausea. Pakistan Journal of Biological Sciences, 14(16), 817-820. https://doi.org/10.3923/pjbs.2011.817.820

Nair, R., & Maseeh, A. (2012). Vitamin D: The 'sunshine' vitamin. J*ournal of Pharmacology & Pharma-*

*cotherapeutics*, 3(2), 118–126. https://doi.org/10.4103/0976-500X.95506

Narendran, S., Nagarathna, R., Narendran, V., Gunasheela, S. & Nagendra, H.R. (2005). Efficacy of yoga on pregnancy outcome. *Alternative and Complementary Medicine*. https://doi.org/10.1089/acm.2005.11.237

National Institute of Mental Health. (n.d.). Perinatal Depression. https://www.nimh.nih.gov/health/publications/perinatal-depression/index.shtml

Nicholas, P., Sharma, A.J., Kim, S.Y. & Hinkle, S.N. (2015). Prevalence and characteristics associated with gestational weight gain adequacy. *Obstetrics & Gynecology*, 125(4), 773-781. https://doi.org/10.1097/AOG.0000000000000739

Partanen, E., Kujala, T., Tervaniemi, M. & Huotilainen, M. (2013) Prenatal music exposure induces long-term neural effects. *PLoS ONE*, 8(10). https://doi.org/10.1371/journal.pone.0078946

Phang, M., Ross, J., Raythatha, J.H., Dissanayake, H.U., McMullan, R.L., Kong, Y., Hyett, J., Gordon, A., Molloy, P. & Skilton, M.R. (2020). Epigenetic aging in newborns: role of maternal diet. *The Amer-*

*ican Journal of Clinical Nutrition*, 111(3), 555–561. https://doi.org/10.1093/ajcn/nqz326

Rice, M. M., Landon, M. B., Varner, M. W., Casey, B. M., Reddy, U. M., Wapner, R. J., Rouse, D. J., Biggio, J. R., Jr, Thorp, J. M., Jr, Chien, E. K., Saade, G., Peaceman, A. M., Blackwell, S. C., VanDorsten, J. P. & Kennedy, E. (2016) Pregnancy-associated hypertension in glucose-intolerant pregnancy and subsequent metabolic syndrome. *Obstetrics and Gynecology*, 127(4), 771–779. https://doi.org/10.1097/AOG.0000000000001353

Royal College of Obstetricians & Gynecologists. (2019). A diet rich in vegetables and fish linked to lower risk of high blood pressure during pregnancy. https://www.rcog.org.uk/en/news/a-diet-rich-in-vegetables-and-fish-linked-to-lower-risk-of-high-blood-pressure-during-pregnancy/

Segre, L.W., Siewert, R.C., Brock, R.L. & O'Hara, M.W. (2013). Emotional distress in mothers of preterm hospitalized infants: A feasibility trial of nurse-delivered treatment. *Journal of Perinatology*, 33(12), 924-928. https://doi.org/10.1038/jp.2013.93

Sit, D., Rothschild, A. & Wisner, K.L. (2006). A

review of postpartum psychosis. *Journal of Women's Health*, 15(4), 352-368. https://doi.org/10.1089/jwh.2006.15.352

University of Calgaray. (2020). Low-calorie sweeteners do not mean low risk for infants. https://www.ucalgary.ca/news/low-calorie-sweeteners-do-not-mean-low-risk-infants#:~:text=Raylene%20Reimer%2C%20PhD%2C%20at%20the,organisms%20that%20inhabit%20the%20intestinal

Van den Heuvel, M., Johannes, M., Henrichs, J. & Bergh, B. (2015). Maternal mindfulness during pregnancy and infant socio-emotional development and temperament: The mediating role of maternal anxiety. *Early Human Development*, 91, 103-108. https://doi.org/1016/j.earlhumdev.2014.12.003

Van den Heuvel, M.L., Donkers, F.C., Winkler, I., Otte, R.A. & Van den Bergh, B.R. (2015). Maternal mindfulness and anxiety during pregnancy affect infants' neural responses to sounds. *Social Cognitive and Affective Neuroscience*, 10(3), 453–460. https://doi.org/10.1093/scan/nsu075

Vieten, C. & Astin, J. (2008). Effects of a mindfulness-based intervention during pregnancy on prenatal stress and mood: Results of a pilot study. *Archives of Women's Mental Health*, 11(1), 67-74. https://doi.org/11.67-74.          10.1007/s00737-008-0214-3

Zhu, Y. & Zhang, C. (2016). Prevalence of Gestational Diabetes and Risk of Progression to Type 2 Diabetes: a Global Perspective. *Current Diabetes Reports*, 16(1), 7. https://doi.org/10.1007/s11892-015-0699-x

Zilcha-Mano, S. & Langer, E. (2016). Mindful attention to variability intervention and successful pregnancy outcomes. *Journal of Clinical Psychology*. https://doi.org/10.1002/jclp.22294